THE ELVIS
IMPERSONATION KIT

THE ELVIS IM

LAURA LEE

PERSONATION KIT

A Step-By-Step Guide To Becoming The King

BLACK DOG
& LEVENTHAL
PUBLISHERS
NEW YORK

Published by
Black Dog & Leventhal Publishers, Inc.
151 West 19th Street
New York, NY 10011

Distributed by
Workman Publishing Company
708 Broadway
New York, NY 10003

Manufactured in China
Cover and Interior design by Andy Taray / Ohioboy Art & Design

ISBN: 1-57912-548-4
ISBN-13: 978-157912-548-6

h g f e d c b a
Library of Congress Cataloging-in-Publication Data available on file.

CONTENTS

THE ELVIS IMPERSONATION KIT

INTRODUCTION:
THE MANY FACES OF ELVIS

Of all human yearnings, it would seem, one of the most universal must be the urge to fling sweaty silk scarves into an audience while croaking an off-key rendition of "Burning Love."

—JOHN FLINN, *SAN FRANCISCO CHRONICLE*

THE MANY FACES OF ELVIS TRIBUTE ARTISTS.

How to impersonate Elvis is a complicated question because of the incredible variety among Elvis performers. Elvises (or Elvi, as they are often known), for the most part, come from one of three basic groups:

1. Tribute artists
2. Comedians/variety acts
3. People who want a little attention at parties

Members of group 1 are usually actors or musicians who are fans of Elvis Presley. They are inspired by a desire to keep the dream alive. They try to be as authentic as possible. The top performers strive for accuracy with the commitment and attention to detail of a Civil War reenactor. They prefer to be referred to as "Elvis tribute artists" or ETAs because they hate the baggage that comes with the label "impersonator." You know, the image of an amateurish, overweight, middle-age man in a bad wig who sings an ear-splitting version of "Don't Be Cruel" in a hotel bar.

Members of group 2 are not trying to invoke the memory of Elvis Presley the performer, but of the cultural phenomenon of Elvis the rock star. Performers in this group often embrace the label "Elvis impersonator," as they are not performing a tribute (sometimes quite the opposite). They often combine the image of Elvis with something unexpected, such as skydiving or roller skating. Wedding Chapel Elvi fit into this category. The real Elvis did not perform weddings. Think of these impersonators as living, breathing velvet paintings of Elvis.

If you bought this book, you're probably part of group 3. To be brutally honest, you are the bane of the existence of some of the members of group 1. Some professional ETAs are embarrassed—not embarrassed to be paying tribute to Elvis Presley, but to be associated with amateur Elvises who gyrate unconvincingly wearing paste-on sideburns and singing in a slightly flat vibrato. Frankly, they are embarrassed by you!

Don't let that stop you. Everyone has the right to indulge his rock star fantasies from time to time, and the greatest rock star fantasy of them all is to be Elvis.

You've got to follow that dream wherever that dream may lead. We've all got some Elvis inside and—black or white, male or female, straight or gay—we all have a right to let him out! You just need a little help to conjure an image of Elvis that doesn't embarrass you or anyone else. That's what this book is all about. Remember, most of the guys who get accolades for their Elvis tributes today started their careers by picking up the karaoke mic on a dare while wearing an ill-fitting Elvis Halloween costume. What's important is the desire and the intention.

ELVIS ILLUSIONIST

The term "Elvis impersonator" has a lot of baggage. People who perform as Elvis have proposed a number of alternatives. Instead of saying "Elvis impersonator," try:

ELVIS TRIBUTE ARTIST

ELVIS ARTIST

ELVIS INTERPRETER

ELVIS PERFORMER

ELVIS ILLUSIONIST

ELVIS AMBASSADOR

ELVIS IMPRESSIONIST

ELVIS STYLIST

PERFORMANCE ARTIST

You may not plan to perform for money, or even to perform like a pro. That's okay. You don't have to have professional aspirations. (Just as you don't need to be a recording artist to sing in your shower, to be a member of American Ballet Theater to dance at a nightclub, or to be a Pulitzer Prize-winner to keep a notebook of poems.) But if you do aspire to professionally portray The King, there should be enough real advice from the experts here to get you started. Have fun.

TRIVIA QUESTION: MOJO NIXON'S SONG "ELVIS IS EVERYWHERE" CLAIMS "ELVIS IS IN EVERYBODY OUT THERE" EXCEPT FOR ONE PERSON, "THE EVIL OPPOSITE OF ELVIS." WHO DID NIXON SAY IS THE "ANTI-ELVIS"?

ANSWER: *Michael J. Fox has got no Elvis in him, according to Nixon—although a better candidate for the title of Anti-Elvis might be Paul Tsongas, whom columnist Molly Ivins once described as having a "minus-zero on the Elvis scale." During the 2004 presidential election campaign, Dan Rather wondered if John Kerry "had enough Elvis in him" to win the election. Apparently he didn't. Kelsey Grammar's Frasier would be the ultimate Anti-Elvis, but he is disqualified because he is fictional. (Kelsey Grammar the actor, however, has a little bit of Elvis in him.)*

CHAPTER 1
GROUND RULES

Anybody who sees Elvis Presley and doesn't want to be like Elvis Presley has got to have something wrong with him.

—BRUCE SPRINGSTEEN WHO, IN 1976, SNUCK ONTO THE GROUNDS OF GRACELAND IN AN UNSUCCESSFUL BID TO MEET HIS IDOL

There are two unbreakable rules when it comes to personifying Elvis for fun or profit:

Rule number 1: You are not Elvis.
Rule number 2: See rule number 1.

In the world of professional Elvis tribute artists, there is one cardinal sin—speaking as though you are The King. Never introduce a song by saying, "I recorded this at Sun Studios" or "I first performed this in 1970." You didn't. Elvis did. You're not Elvis.

"Everyone has to be their own personal self," says Nashville-based Elvis artist Travis LeDoyt. "It's sad when somebody has lost that and is pretending to be Elvis all the time. That also gives a bad name to [Elvis tribute artists] because it's silly to walk around and go in a restaurant dressed like Elvis when you're just going out to eat."

If you have any doubts about your identity, take the following quiz:

ARE YOU CRAZY OR AN ELVIS IMPERSONATOR?

CRAZY	ELVIS IMPERSONATOR
You believe you are Elvis.	You believe you are a guy named Steve who does a fairly good imitation of Presley's voice on "Hound Dog."
You go to Graceland because you live there and own it.	You go to Graceland to gain insight into Elvis Presley and to pay respect to the greatest rock star who ever lived.
When members of the Graceland staff try to stop you from entering, you tell them they're fired.	You pester the staff with many questions about Elvis hoping to learn something you can incorporate into your act.
You sit down in the jungle room and decide to redecorate it in an Alaskan theme.	You burn through half a roll of film taking pictures of the jungle room.
When the police arrive, you warn them you have a black belt in karate and that Nixon made you a "federal agent-at-large" in the Bureau of Narcotics and Dangerous Drugs.	You ask a security guard for directions to a good place to stop for lunch before heading to the gift shop for a few souvenirs.
As you are taken away in handcuffs, you ask to make your one phone call to Col. Tom Parker.	As you drive away, you feel joyous and especially inspired to give a great performance on Saturday.

If any of your answers are close to those in the left-hand column, put down this book. You can find what you need in the Yellow Pages under "psychologists and psychiatrists."

Elvis impersonators do not go to the grocery store in their white jumpsuits or ask their neighbors to jump and squeal as they mow the lawn. They're just folks who would rather earn a living performing as Elvis than by working in a cubicle. How crazy is that?

One of the things that makes Elvis an icon is his ambiguity: he is both white and black, he is strong, masculine and swaggering, yet he is also tender and sensitive ... He's also a white working-class man who becomes this incredible icon yet remains true to his humble roots. Yet he's rich, so he's neither one nor the other.

—JEREMY WALLACH, ASSISTANT PROFESSOR, DEPARTMENT OF POPULAR CULTURE, BOWLING GREEN STATE UNIVERSITY

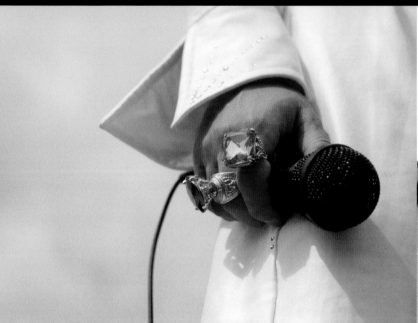

By acting as Elvis, the impersonator taps into a powerful image with a whole collection of associations. Put on that Elvis suit, and immediately people see you differently. The costume, the sideburns, the scarves invoke a whole group of automatic responses (click-whrrr). In an Elvis costume, you can bypass anonymity and move straight to rock-star status. As Brian Simpson, a Canadian Elvis, put it: "At the Collingwood Elvis festival there were 12,000 people a day watching the performance. These are guys that have never sung before more than 40 people at a karaoke bar, now they're standing in front of 12,000 people. There are actual bands that never get to stand in front of 12,000 people." That's the power of Elvis.

But couldn't the same be said for many other artists? Certainly there are other rock stars who have attained a mythic status in our popular culture. So why do people ask for weddings performed by Elvis and not by, say, John Lennon?

Unlike other dead rock stars, Elvis seems to contain multitudes. He is everything and its opposite at once. He has so many facets

that everyone finds something to relate to—this, say scholars, is why so many people feel free to take on the Elvis persona. Sure, there was Beatlemania and there are Doors tribute bands, but are there Indonesian Jim Morrison impersonators? Are there African-American Kurt Cobain tribute artists? Are there Filipino Jimi Hendrixes, Norwegian Jerry Garcias, or Chinese Janis Joplins? Perhaps a few, but with Elvis you can be guaranteed that any subgroup or culture has at least one Elvis, probably several.

GOVERNOR BILL CLINTON PLAYS SAX ON "THE ARSENIO HALL SHOW," JUNE 3, 1992.

CLOSET ELVIS—BILL CLINTON

In 1970, a psychic named George Dareos predicted, "One day the South will nominate Elvis Presley to become president of the United States." That didn't happen. Bill Clinton, the forty-second president of the United States, may be as close as we'll ever get to having Elvis behind the desk in the Oval Office. Clinton let a little of his Elvis escape when he appeared on **The Arsenio Hall Show** during the 1992 election campaign and played "Heartbreak Hotel" on the saxophone. Clinton also sang "Don't Be Cruel" on a New York radio talk show, discussed his lifelong fascination with Presley in a **Newsweek** interview, and was code-named "Elvis" by the Secret Service.

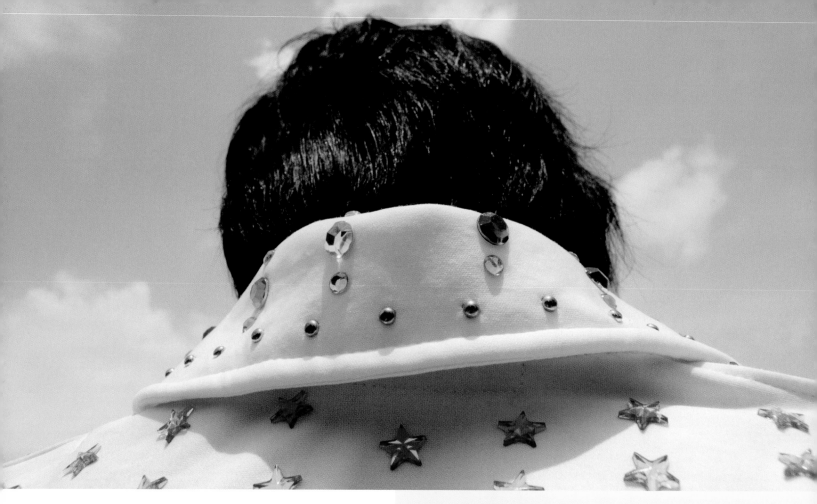

TRIVIA QUESTION: WHICH OF THESE IS NOT A REAL ELVIS PERFORMER?

A. Elvis Herselvis—Lesbian Elvis from San Francisco (with backing band the Straight White Males)

B. Jukka Ammondt—of Helsinki, Finland, who recorded Elvis hits in Latin

C. Rex Redhair—Navajo Elvis

D. Elvis Priestly—An independent Anglican priest who leads church services as Elvis

E. The Blue Elvis Group

ANSWER: *E. To the best of our knowledge, there is no Blue Elvis Group. … yet.*

In December 1956, *Cosmopolitan* posed the question: "What Is an Elvis Presley?"

This is the question that every aspiring Elvis—whether he plays Elvis straight or as a parody—has to answer for himself. What exactly is an Elvis? With so many permutations on the basic Elvis theme, what is the essential quality of Elvisness?

Perhaps, in the course of trying to better imitate The King, we'll figure it out.

ELVIS AND POLITICS

- "Ladies and Gentlemen, whenever I go to the polls to vote for a mayor, I always ask myself what is his economic policy. … How does he stand on the environment. … And can he sing 'Love Me Tender'?" —David Letterman introducing Bruce Borders, an Elvis tribute artist who was elected mayor of Jacksonville, Indiana.

- In northern England, Eddie Vee, "The Yorkshire Elvis," ran for Parliament in 2001 on a platform calling for an Elvis memorial garden in York. He lost.

- Elvis impersonator Dean Vegas once ran for mayor in Queensland, Australia, and vowed to govern in a white jumpsuit if elected.

- In 1992, in Wisconsin, the Democratic nominee for the Senate, Russell D. Feingold, ran a TV spot with a bogus supermarket tabloid heading reading, "Elvis Endorses Feingold." Just one week after Feingold's upset victory over his two primary opponents, the Republican incumbent, Senator Robert Kasten, began running a thirty-second commercial featuring an Elvis impersonator.

- During the 1992 presidential campaign, Republicans hired Elvis impersonators to follow the Clinton tour buses. They thought that the association of Clinton and Elvis would be a negative in the public's mind. Turns out they misjudged that one.

> "Elvis performers are like VHS tapes. If someone copies from an original, you have a good quality tape. If you copy from another performer, you have a copy of a copy, a second-generation Elvis performer. And too many copy from a copy of a copy of a copy. Don't be like that. If you use things others do, and copy how they do it, you aren't doing Elvis justice."
>
> —JAMIE AARON KELLY, QUOTED IN *WALK A MILE IN THEIR SHOES* BY JUNE MOORE AND MELODY SANDERS

CHAPTER 3
AN ELVIS
EDUCATION

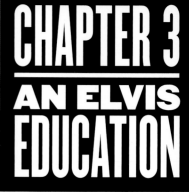

There is no Elvis University and no single governing body that qualifies you to be Elvis. Professional Elvis impersonators are mostly self-taught and come to it from all backgrounds. Your homework assignment, should you choose to accept it, is to go out and rent a few essential Elvis Presley videos. It's vital that you see the ones from the period you wish to dramatize, but you may also want to rent the others to watch the Presley progression. Besides, it's fun. There are dozens from which to choose, but there are a few that no self-respecting Elvis performer should go without seeing. Call this Elvis 101.

MUST-VIEWS:

ELVIS—THE GREAT PERFORMANCES BOXED SET

This is a collection of footage from various periods in Elvis's career. You can find all the essential early television appearances in one place here. The set contains a number of documentaries and biographical films that include Elvis's early television appearances. You can get the set at any video store or even your local library.

JAILHOUSE ROCK

If you rent one Elvis movie make it this one, for the "Jailhouse Rock" dance segment alone.

'68 COMEBACK SPECIAL

This television special touted as Elvis's "return" to rock and roll after a decade of uninspiring film work has become a genre all its own. Many ETAs make a career out of this one television moment. Your Elvis education is incomplete if you haven't seen it.

ELVIS—ALOHA FROM HAWAII

One and a half billion people watched "Elvis—Aloha from Hawaii" broadcast by satellite in 1973. This is the one image most casual observers have of the late Elvis. Any 1970s ETA will be measured against this performance. You need to see it.

OPTIONAL VIEWING:

BLUE HAWAII

The plot of this 1961 feature is a bit thin, but it is a perennial favorite and Elvis's biggest box-office success. It features Angela Lansbury as Elvis's mom (she would have to have been ten years old when she gave birth to him). This is feel-good cinema at its finest, colorful, beautiful scenery, women in bikinis, "Can't Help Falling in Love," "Rock-A-Hula Baby," and Elvis—on a surfboard. What more could you want?

G.I. BLUES

The title number from this film is oft imitated. If you want to add the GI look to your act, you'll have to take a look at this movie.

VIVA LAS VEGAS

Elvis's dance numbers with Ann-Margret and the rousing theme number feature prominently in Elvis lore. You probably won't want to hire an Ann-Margret look-alike to dance with you, but you should see this to know what everyone is talking about.

IMPORTANT DATES IN THE LIFE OF THE KING
These are the dates and events that every would-be King must know. Commit them to memory.

JANUARY 8, 1935—Elvis is born in Tupelo, MS.

SEPTEMBER 12, 1948—Elvis moves to Memphis, TN.

JULY 5, 1954—Elvis makes his first commercial recording at Sun Studios in Memphis.

MARCH 13, 1956—Elvis's first album, *Elvis Presley,* is released.

SEPTEMBER 9, 1956—Elvis makes his first appearance on *The Ed Sullivan Show.*

NOVEMBER 15, 1956—Elvis's first feature film, *Love Me Tender,* is released.

MARCH 24, 1958—Elvis enters the army.

AUGUST 14, 1958—Elvis's mother, Gladys, dies.

MARCH 5, 1960—Elvis is discharged from the army.

MAY 1, 1967—Elvis marries Priscilla in Las Vegas.

FEBRUARY 1, 1968—Lisa Marie Presley is born.

DECEMBER 3, 1968—Elvis performs the "Comeback Special," his first live performance in seven years.

JULY 31, 1969—Elvis makes his first appearance in Las Vegas in thirteen years at the International Hotel.

DECEMBER 21, 1970—Elvis visits the White House and meets President Richard Nixon.

JANUARY 14, 1973—"Elvis—Aloha from Hawaii" is the first worldwide satellite broadcast.

OCTOBER 9, 1973—Elvis and Priscilla divorce.

JUNE 26, 1977—Elvis performs his last concert at Market Square Arena, in Indianapolis, IN.

AUGUST 16, 1977—Elvis dies at Graceland at age forty-two.

It's very hard to live up to an image.

—ELVIS PRESLEY, 1972

THESE ELVIS STAMPS, SHOWING THE VARIOUS VERSIONS OF THE KING, WERE RELEASED BY THE TINY ISLAND OF ST. VINCENT IN AUGUST 1992.

Elvis was many things to many people—rock star, movie star, crooner, mama's boy, churchgoer, self-parodist, dangerous purveyor of moral decay, wholesome role model, patriotic army recruit, bloated example of celebrity excess, object of worship and devotion. . . .

For our purposes, we'll explore only three and a half primary Elvis types:

1. '70s Elvis—By far the most distinctive and popular Elvis to impersonate
2. '50s Elvis—The sexiest and most challenging Elvis
3. Movie Star Elvis—Very few people choose to impersonate this Elvis because of the expense of hiring a film crew.
3½. Gospel Elvis—This is not really a "period," more of a state of mind.

So, which Elvis will you be? In many ways, you do not choose your Elvis, your Elvis chooses you. The third ground rule is:

Rule number 3: Act your age.

This rule is a bit more flexible than ground rules 1 and 2. As with sports, some performers manage to compete with much younger people well into their forties, but they are the exception. Most aspiring Elvises don't have the physical wherewithal to perform young Elvis after the gray hairs start sneaking in (Elvis couldn't do it). They're forced to slowly shift from the transitional "'68 Comeback Special" Elvis into the jumpsuit-wearing Vegas icon.

"You portray the era with which your age closely matches Elvis's," says Brian Simpson, a Canadian ETA who teaches an actual course in impersonation called Elvis 101. "I am thirty-eight years old. That would put me in the Aloha jumpsuit period. For me to dress up to look like I was doing Elvis in the 1950s onstage now would be no different than him trying to do it himself. It just wouldn't fit. It's important, if you're going to portray him, you want to portray him in the best light you can, and it's not complimentary or at all believable to be a forty-five-year-old gentleman trying to represent Elvis in 1957 when he was twenty years old."

And what happens when you turn forty-two? Do you thereafter portray the ghost of Elvis? Of course not. There are hundreds of folks out there playing Elvis at an age he never actually attained; in fact, there are now people who have been performing as Elvis longer than Elvis did, and that's okay, say the experts. If Elvis were alive today he would be seventy. Funny how time slips away. We never got to see a senior citizen Elvis, but that doesn't mean we can't imagine one, and many performers refuse to name an upper age limit for Elvis performance.

"I don't think there's an age limit as long as people are willing to pay you to do it, and as long as you can maintain the look," says Jerome Marion, an Elvis from Illinois. "I think you can do this well into your fifties, maybe even sixty years old if you still have the energy and the charisma. Elvis is going to be around for a long time to come and I hope to do this as long as my jumpsuits fit and my voice holds out."

SIMON LUXTON, FROM ENGLAND, DOES A LITTLE SOUL SEARCHING.

CHAPTER 5
'70S ELVIS
AKA VEGAS ELVIS, JUMPSUIT ELVIS, ALOHA ELVIS

Most [Elvis impersonators] don't really look like him, but that doesn't matter, because the iconic Elvis has been reduced to a few basic and instantly recognizable elements: sequined white jumpsuit with elephant bell-bottoms and a high collar with shoulder-wide wings, girder-sided silver glasses, and masses of glittering rings on the fingers.

—JANE AND MICHAEL STERN, *THE ENCYCLOPEDIA OF BAD TASTE*

Chronology be damned. We begin our journey in the 1970s because this is the incontestable image that springs to mind when you hear the words "Elvis impersonator." It was the decade in which Elvis became "The King." This is the era of the complex and troubled, larger than life character, so easy to caricature, emulate or parody.

In 1992, when Americans were given an option to select an image of Elvis Presley for a U.S. stamp, nearly 1.2 million people sent ballots to the United States Postal Service, and the winner was clear: more than 75 percent of voters preferred the young Elvis image to the older one. Yet you wouldn't know it by watching Elvis tribute artists.

Whether you love him or hate him, the tragicomic theatrical "King" is so much fun to imitate. Elvis fans find great nobility in the way he continued to devote such energy and love to his performance, even as his health began to fail. They pay tribute to this era because it is the last image he left us with—the one we're not ready to let go. His detractors, meanwhile, milk this Elvis for obvious humor.

THE POSSIBILITIES FOR THE VEGAS ELVIS ARE ENDLESS.

"A lot of people going to Elvis impersonations are doing it with their tongue in cheek and an elbow in the ribs. That may not be true of all the performers but a lot of the people are doing it; and, let's face it, the Vegas Elvis is funnier," said Robert Thompson, former president of the International Popular Culture Association. "Secondly, early Elvis depended on this impeccable sense of timing—the way his body looked was very crucial—you had to have a body that would live up to that. By the time you get to the later things, the movements are a little easier to imitate because they're not as complex, the body type is much easier to imitate—a lot more people are built like a Vegas Elvis. And the music itself: when you get to the Vegas years, Elvis was performing something that was very close to being a parody of himself."

The irony is that as Elvis's dancing became more subdued, and his physical shape more … shall we say … easy to imitate, the vocal difficulty of the music increased. So if you think you'll get out of having to rehearse by choosing to portray the Vegas Elvis, think again. You just have different challenges—not the least of which is figuring out how to move around in a heavy, bejeweled costume with fringe.

Don't underestimate the musical rehearsal time you'll need. The big emotional ballads such as "American Trilogy" are harder to sing than they seem. You can't get away with a little break in the voice when you're singing such lyrics as "Glory, Glory Hallelujah!"

RITCHIC NEWTON, FROM GERMANY, KILLS AS VEGAS ELVIS.

People have this misconception that Elvis was fat. When actually he was only bloated from the drugs and it was only the last two and a half or three years of his life. You get these people who weigh five hundred pounds and they put on a jumpsuit and think they can be Elvis, and I think that's the biggest thing people get wrong. Pretty soon that's their opinion not only of Elvis but of other tribute artists. I start hearing, "You should be heavier."

—JOHN LOOS, WYOMING-BASED ETA

Okay, let's deal with the elephant in the jumpsuit on the table— Elvis and his weight. As he got older, Elvis had a harder time keeping a trim figure. Do you have the same waist size at age forty that you had at twenty-five? … I didn't think so.

What was Elvis's "real" weight? Well, in the beginning he weighed five pounds. It was all uphill from there. At the peak of his career, he weighed between 165 and 170. When he came out of the army, he weighed about 175. A year later, he weighed 180. As Elvis reached his mid-thirties, his frame took on an extra 30 pounds. He was about to film the movie *Clambake* and the studio ordered him to lose the weight in a hurry. Diet pills became a staple of the Presley diet. (The public is apparently more accepting of thin addicts than of nonaddicts with a few extra pounds on them.) After that, his weight went up and down as Elvis gave in to his cravings for freshly made banana pudding and the starchy Southern cooking of his youth, and then fought against their effects. At the very end of his life, he weighed 260 pounds.

Although people associate the American Eagle costume Elvis wore in the TV special "Aloha from Hawaii" with his being overweight, Elvis had actually gotten down to a trim 168 to look good for the world. The book *Elvis Fashion,* written in cooperation with Graceland, goes out of its way to dispel the myth of the fat Elvis. The descriptions of most of the late-period Elvis costumes say things like, "This costume was so slim we had trouble finding a mannequin for it."

Elvis fans can get a bit touchy about the "fat Elvis" stereotype, and, for the most part, they don't want to see a fat Elvis. So if you were hoping that you could take up Elvis impersonation as an excuse to go off your diet, sorry, you're out of luck.

Performing as Elvis is, in itself, a good exercise regimen. A sensible diet, weight training, sit-ups, jogging, and all the rest are highly recommended. Just avoid Elvis's own excesses in your attempts to lose the pounds—diet pills are not recommended, nor is the "yogurt diet," wrapping yourself with plastic wrap under your costume, being injected with the urine of a pregnant woman, or the "sleep diet"—a Las Vegas doctor once prescribed Elvis enough medication to sleep for weeks under the theory that if he didn't get out of bed, he couldn't eat and he'd lose weight. (Avoiding Elvis's excesses is good rule of thumb in general.)

Elvis, if you believe what you read, ate more food than any other man who ever lived. ... No doubt, the man had a healthy appetite; he always did; and in the final years, his metabolism slowed and trapped him. But what's wonderful about the preposterous accounts of his binges is that in the telling they became an everyday Elvis feat. If Elvis ever did anything once—and anyone saw him do it—it was then written (in its most lurid and exaggerated form) as part of the superhuman Elvis legend.

—JANE AND MICHAEL STERN, *ELVIS WORLD*

Late in his life, Elvis did everything big: he dressed big, he sang big, he lived big, he crashed big, and he ate big. If you want to keep in shape to play Elvis, you should not try to imitate Elvis's diet. It is impossible to maintain an Elvis figure while eating like Elvis—even Elvis couldn't do it. Yet if all the tales about his dietary excesses are true, it is amazing that Elvis was able to stay as thin as he did. Surely Elvis had superhuman metabolism.

Just in case you value lifestyle authenticity over pants-size authenticity, here is a little sample of what The King reportedly consumed.

Elvis was a man of simple tastes. He favored the country cooking of his youth—fried cornmeal mush, corned beef and potato hash, black-eyed peas, sweet potato pie, and grits were favorites. He loved glazed doughnuts, burnt bacon, and anything cooked in butter.

Elvis's most famous favorite snack was a peanut butter and banana sandwich fried in butter. To make this delicacy, take two pieces of bread, one banana, mashed, and a jar of peanut butter. Spread the mashed banana on one slice of bread, the peanut butter on the other, put them together, and slather the outside of the bread with butter, then fry up the whole thing in a pan. It's a protein-rich snack with only 745 calories—give or take.

To satisfy his late-night cravings for sweets, Elvis had a standing order that banana pudding be prepared daily and that fresh brownies always be on hand.

It was said that in the 1970s he would eat a 5:00 p.m. breakfast of six large eggs, burnt bacon, and half a pound of sausage, plus twelve buttermilk biscuits. He also developed more discerning

tastes as he got older, and eggs Benedict was a favorite of his Vegas stays.

He was known to polish off a dozen cheeseburgers at a time, and have room for a gallon of ice cream for dessert. He had a soft spot for "Fool's Gold" sandwiches, which consisted of a jar of strawberry jam, a jar of peanut butter, and a pound of crisp fried bacon served on a whole loaf of bread split down the middle. Rumor is that Elvis could eat two in a sitting.

If you want to sample something Elvis liked that won't kill you, try a big plate of sliced beefsteak tomatoes. He loved 'em.

A number of cookbooks have been published full of Elvis Presley favorites. Pick one up in a used bookstore for hearty meat loaf and fried chicken recipes. *The Girl's Guide to Elvis,* by Kim Adelman, includes a few recipes for lower-calorie versions of Elvis's faves.

It's hard to get into a one-piece suit without hurting yourself.

—ELVIS PRESLEY

ELVIS SUITS FROM *LEFT TO RIGHT*:
DRAGON, SUNDIAL, PEACOCK, FLAME,
TIGER, AND RAINBOW.

If you hear the expression "Blue Prehistoric Bird" and immediately think "Elvis costume," you may already be an Elvis impersonator.

The names of some of his other Vegas period costumes were: American Eagle, Black Eagle, Blue Aztec, Blue Braid, Blue Swirl, Burning Love, Flame, Gypsy, Indian, Inca Gold Leaf, King of Spades, Mad Tiger, Mexican Sundial, Nail-Studded Suit, Peacock, Read Eagle, Red Lion, Sundial, Tiffany, White Eagle, and, of course, White Prehistoric Bird.

The late Elvis look was said to be based on Elvis's love of the comic book hero Captain Marvel, who turned into a super hero when he yelled "Shazaam!" This is also what you might say (or at least the first part of it) when you get the bill for the suit. An authentic late-period Elvis costume can cost anywhere from $2,000 to $4,000. If you can't afford it, be another Elvis. Nothing looks worse to a serious Elvis or Elvis-ophile than an ill-fitted, mock-Elvis costume.

It is a truism in the ETA world that the value of your show correlates to the value of your costuming. "Emerald Elvis" Mark Leen says he has a $70,000 wardrobe. "I'm probably the best customer to B&K Enterprises. People cut corners, but every time I pick up the phone to B&K, I'm spending $10,000."

B&K Enterprises is the biggest manufacturer of late Elvis wear (check the Resources section). Just about every "big-time" Elvis tribute artist gets his suits from them. B&K is the only organization with the original Elvis costume patterns and permission from the original designers to reproduce them. If you're going for authenticity, this is where you have to shop.

To give you an idea of what you're paying for, the popular Aloha Liberty Eagle takes about nine hours to cut and sew. Putting on all those beads and studs can take another fifty-five hours. It takes nine or ten hours just to complete the belt, and it takes three people to do it. Now that you have a new appreciation for the workmanship of the jumpsuit, let's look at some of the great 1970s costumes.

THAT'S THE WAY IT IS
It is said Elvis was inspired by his karate gear to switch to jumpsuits: In the 1970 MGM documentary *Elvis: That's the Way it Is,* he wore a relatively simple and modest jumpsuit. This is as close to a bargain, 70s costume as you'll get. He wore it with a macramé belt, also good for the '70s Elvis on a budget.

FIRE LOOK
This dramatic fire-themed suit was worn by Elvis beginning in 1976. It has a bold flame design on the back, the raised collar, the studded belt, and on the wide kick pleats. Smokin'.

THE DRAGON
This elaborately embroidered jumpsuit features a dragon with a tail twisting its way down the leg all the way to the elephant bell-bottoms with a gold kick pleat.

WARNING: STAY AWAY FROM SPANDEX. BARBARA DEL PIANO, A FEMALE ELVIS WHO GOES BY THE STAGE NAME "BELVIS," STARTED OUT IN A "GOD-AWFUL SPANDEX COSTUME." HER ADVICE: "THE LAST THING YOU WANT TO DO IS PUT SPANDEX ON SOMEBODY WHO'S FIVE FOOT SEVEN AND TWO HUNDRED POUNDS."

BELIEVE IT OR NOT ... REPLICAS OF THE COSTUMES GO ON TOUR. B&K ENTERPRISES OFFERS A TOURING MALL DISPLAY WITH RE-CREATIONS OF FAMOUS ELVIS OUTFITS. CALL IT THE ELVIS COSTUME IMPERSONATORS TOUR.

YOU'VE GOT TO FIGHT ... FOR YOUR RIGHT ... TO EL-VIS.

When David Groh, of Seattle, a part-time actor and ballroom dance instructor, took a job as a taxi driver to make ends meet, he decided to have fun with his job. Instead of wearing the black slacks and blue shirt that city dress codes required of cab drivers, Groh piloted his cab as Elvis. Monday through Wednesday he dressed as '50s Elvis and, on weekends, he got behind the wheel decked out in full Aloha gear, complete with cape. He played Elvis tunes on the tape deck, and after long trips he would drape the necks of his passengers with leis. He even got himself ordained as a minister in the Universal Life Church so he could marry couples while dressed as Elvis. Not only did the passengers have more fun, but Groh also got bigger tips! Inevitably the press got word that there was a taxi-driving Elvis in town, and Groh was featured on the radio and in local magazines. The city was not amused, and he was fined and told to follow the dress code or else. Groh appealed the fine and filed a lawsuit. In December 2003, the Seattle City Council revised its regulations so that drivers would be allowed to sport costumes. After the vote Groh said, "Uh, thank you, thank you very much."

DON OBUSEK IN HIS AMERICAN EAGLE SUIT.

TIP

HEALTH AND SAFETY TIP: TAKE YOUR COSTUME TO THE THEATER IN A SUIT CARRIER RATHER THAN WEARING IT TO YOUR GIG. IT IS NOT YOUR LOUNGING-AROUND WEAR, IT'S A THEATRICAL COSTUME. IF YOU DRIVE TO WORK IN YOUR ELVIS UNIFORM, YOU MAY SPILL COFFEE ON IT—NOT RECOMMENDED FOR A $4,000 SUIT. WORSE, YOU COULD SLAM THE CAR DOOR ON YOUR CAPE OR TASSELS. THIS IS POTENTIALLY QUITE DANGEROUS AND IT IS THE TYPE OF ACCIDENT THAT WOULD BE TRAGIC FOR YOU—BUT FUNNY TO A LOT OF OTHER PEOPLE. IMAGINE WHAT YOUR LOCAL MORNING RADIO SHOW HOSTS WOULD DO WITH THAT NEWS ITEM.

THE AMERICAN EAGLE

Perhaps the most sought-after and the most expensive suit was the embroidered and bejeweled American Eagle jumpsuit with matching cape. The original calf-length cape was so heavy that Elvis couldn't perform in it. In fact, he could barely stand in it. According to Julie Mundy's *Elvis Fashion,* when Elvis tried it on for the first time, Joe Esposito, Elvis's number one aide from 1960 till 1977, had to make an emergency call to designer Bill Belew, saying the singer was "lying on the floor roaring with laughter."

AZTEC SUNDIAL

This was one of the most impressive costumes that Elvis commissioned, but unfortunately it has such bad associations that few tribute artists wear it. (It's also very expensive.) The suit featured elaborate mosaic work in gold, silver, and copper in a traditional Aztec design. It was truly stunning. Elvis actually wore it more than any other costume, and he had two of them in different sizes to accommodate his fluctuating weight. But most fans remember it, if they remember it at all, as the costume he wore just before his death, when he was bloated, exhausted, and unstable. It's just not the memory most fans want to celebrate.

WHAT'S UNDER THAT JUMPSUIT?

When wearing a form-fitting jumpsuit, take care to wear the appropriate underwear. Nothing is more embarrassing than an Elvis with visible panty lines. Elvis wore what designer Bill Belew described as "elastic undershorts." Guys may want to invest in a dance belt; not only doesn't it show under the tightest costume, it also ensures that all your parts stop jiggling when you do.

VASU SANGSINGKEO OF THAILAND IN THE SUNDIAL SUIT.

> I invested 1,140 hours of my life into making this suit. I hand-stitched 22,405 individual beads and sequins on it, double-knotted. ... The total cost in the materials amounted to only $397.86. However, if you go by, say, $9.00 an hour in labor, this suit costs someone $10,240.00 in labor. And if you add in the materials, its total would be $10,637.86. This was not a cheap, fast, easy suit to make.
>
> —CATT, DAUGHTER OF AN ETA, ON SEWING A REPLICA AMERICAN EAGLE JUMPSUIT, FROM HER WEB PAGE, WWW.THECATTBOX.COM

If you have a skill for sewing, and a bit of time, there's nothing to stop you from making your own costume. Fringe, beads, and cloth can be purchased at any fabric store. But your homemade costume may not be much cheaper than the kinds you buy, when you figure in the value of your time. The professionals have got Elvis suit production down to a science. If it takes them sixty to eighty hours to complete an elaborate costume, you can conservatively expect to spend twice as much time on your costume. But it is a labor of love, and the creation of your own costume can be a great way to express your creativity.

Pua Maunu, a Hawaiian artist, created a beautiful and distinctive version of an Elvis suit for her husband, Leonard Johnson, an Alaskan Native American and a somewhat reluctant Elvis impersonator (he was recruited for the job as a model for Maunu's Tlingit Elvis costume). Among the four or five Elvises in Juneau, Alaska, Johnson is unique. He only lip-synchs, but the fusion of Native American art and Elvis has made him a local celebrity.

So far, Johnson hasn't combined his Elvis-inspired wear with traditional Native American dance, but he has gotten many requests to do so, and he says he might try it in the future.

The costume, which was recently on display in the Juneau-Douglas City Museum, incorporates intricate painting, beadwork, and feathers. The back of the cape features an eagle, the symbol of Johnson's tribal clan, painted in a traditional Tlingit style.

"Who would have thought that Elvis and the Northwest Coast go together so beautifully?" Jane Lindsay, director of the Juneau-Douglas City Museum, said.

BEGINNER'S MISTAKES: STAY AWAY FROM SEQUINS. BUTCH POLSTON OF B&K ENTERPRISES SAID TO LESLIE RUBINOWSKI, AUTHOR OF **IMPERSONATING ELVIS,** "NONE OF ELVIS PRESLEY'S COSTUMES HAD SEQUINS ON THEM—NOT ONE OF THEM HAD A SEQUIN ON THEM."

TIP

LEONARD JOHNSON POSING IN THE TLINGIT INSPIRED CAPE MADE BY HIS WIFE, PUA MAUNU.

Anybody who does Elvis, it could be Bob Dole up there—if he's doing Elvis, there'll be women coming down to get their scarf, so you better be ready.

—RICK MARINO, QUOTED IN *I, ELVIS* BY WILLIAM MCCRANOR HENDERSON

FEMALE ELVIS TRIBUTE ARTISTS KNOWN AS "THE GRACELINERS" SHOW OFF THEIR GLITTERING ELVIS SCARVES.

The scarf is more than just a piece of costuming. It is an essential part of the show. The scarf brings the audience into the performance. Most women don't feel they can take on the Elvis persona (although some do), but they still want to play a part, and if you forget your scarves, you rob them of the opportunity.

Elvis didn't just hand out scarves—he bestowed them on his fans with a kiss, he patted his brow with them, he used them to wipe the perspiration from his chest, and he even took handkerchiefs and scarves from women in the audience to pat down his brow and hand back again. The recipients of the scarves got a little bit of Elvis, a little of his chemistry, his DNA—just a little sample of Elvis's body.

"Big sequined Elvis or not, this was sweat that came out of Elvis and that still meant something," said pop culture expert Robert Thompson. "That people would desire the sweat from an Elvis impersonator is probably more an issue of, 'This is part of the convention of what this game is about.'"

The bestowing of the scarves came into Elvis's act in Las Vegas in 1970. That summer, he began ordering scarves by the dozens from IC Costumes in Los Angeles. It wouldn't be long before he was ordering them by the hundreds.

So there is no question: if you do a 1970s Elvis, you need scarves. But this need not be a huge expense. A number of people make a

ELVIS TRIBUTE ARTIST, DAVID LEE, HANDING OUT SCARVES TO HIS AUDIENCE.

CLONING ELVIS?

Could those sweaty scarves that Elvis gave away as souvenirs be used to clone The King? In theory, they could. Sweat has some DNA, which is a very stable molecule. Fragments of sweat that are thousands of years old have been found in archeological artifacts, especially if the artifacts have been kept dry or free from microbes that can cause decay. So if a scarf Elvis actually sweated on were properly preserved and there were enough of it there, theoretically it could be used to make a clone of Elvis. Don't think no one has thought of this. A group called "Americans for Cloning Elvis" started a petition asking the U.S. government to change its policies on human cloning so a new Elvis could be born. But here's the thing: Even if it were possible to make a clone of Elvis from a sweaty scarf or a hair clipping, it would still not be Elvis. Cloning could never reproduce the environment or social forces that made Elvis who he was. What is more, Dan Goldowitz, director for the Center of Excellence for Genomics and Bioinformatics, told the *Report Newsmagazine*, "We can do it. The only problem is that there's a tendency for genetic abnormality to occur. ... We'd get an Elvis, but maybe he would just want to deliver the mail."

TIP: DON'T MISS OUT ON A MARKETING OPPORTUNITY. IF YOU PERFORM PROFESSIONALLY, HAVE THE NAME OF YOUR ACT AND CONTACT INFORMATION PRINTED ON FABRIC LABELS. SEW THEM TO THE INSIDE OF THE SCARVES. THUS THE SCARVES YOU GIVE AWAY ACT AS HIGHLY EFFECTIVE BUSINESS CARDS.

decent part-time living just sewing scarves for Elvis performers. His scarves were made of fine silk, but you can probably get a reasonable facsimile of an Elvis scarf at a department store or even the Salvation Army.

If you have lots of extra money lying around, you might try to purchase an "authentic" Elvis scarf on eBay. There's a catch, though: most of the "authentic" scarves aren't.

First off, souvenir scarves were sold at stands at Elvis concerts. These are "authentic" souvenirs, but not authentic scarves that Elvis wore.

"Most of the scarves we're asked to appraise are those," says Elvis memorabilia expert Jerry Osborne, "though most of the people usually say 'Elvis gave me this one.' Then we settle the matter by asking if his name is stitched on the scarf. Usually it is, and that makes it a souvenir scarf."

Truly authentic scarves—the ones Elvis wore and gave away—have no embroidery on them. No one knows exactly how many he draped on his fans. Not surprisingly, this makes it very easy for people to sell fakes. Because it is so hard to know for sure if a scarf is authentic, the collector's price is lower than you might expect—about $100.

CHAPTER 11
'70S ACCESSORIES: SHOES AND JEWELRY

You can do anything, but lay off my blue suede shoes.

—ELVIS PRESLEY

LEFT TO RIGHT: ACTOR BILL MCGRATH SHOWS OFF HIS TCB CHARM. / ELVIS BLING. / WHITE SHOES MAKE THE OUTFIT.

Proper accessories—shoes, belts, glasses, and jewelry—are the mark of a serious ETA. Chances are, from the audience, no one will really notice if you have an appropriate necklace. You can get away with a fair amount of cheating here, but paying attention to the details adds up. It's picked up on a subconscious level, and getting enough of the details right sets you apart from the pretenders.

First, let's talk about Elvis's jewelry. Even in the 1950s, Elvis had a weakness for the flashy stuff. One of his first big purchases when he started to make money was a gold ring with the initials EP set in diamonds for $185 (close to $1,300 in today's currency).

Throughout his career he continued to have jewelry custom made, much of it incorporating his initials or the letters TCB, an abbreviated form of Elvis's motto, "Taking Care of Business."

Elvis's massive rings were part of his costume but they were not "costume jewelry." They were decked out in thousands of dollars' worth of gold and gemstones. He had trouble keeping them because he just couldn't refrain from giving them away, but also because they were sometimes grabbed as souvenirs by overly enthusiastic fans. Elvis took to wearing bandages around the ends of his fingers, to make the rings harder for fans to pull off when he reached down from the stage and shook their hands. Theft of Elvis's jewels continues to this day. In 2004, about $325,000 worth of Elvis Presley's jewelry was stolen from the Elvis-A-Rama Museum, in Las Vegas.

There was a time when TCB knockoffs were hard to find, but thanks to the Internet you can pick up cheap replicas of Elvis's jewels all over the place. The same is true of Elvis-inspired shoes.

Nothing spoils the look of a $4,000 jumpsuit more than a pair of dirty sneakers. Elvis rarely wore them. And forget the blue suede shoes—what you need are white boots. You may be able to find authentic '70s boots at a secondhand store but if you can't, try the Internet. There are enough Elvis tribute artists today, that a supply industry has grown to serve them. What would have required major scrounging in 1990 is a click away today. If you don't manage to get online in time, head to a tuxedo shop and rent a pair of white shoes. Your bell-bottoms should disguise the fact that they are not boots—at least until you do that karate kick. By then, with any luck, the crowd will be so dazzled that they won't care.

IT'S ALL ABOUT ME

Elvis loved to incorporate references to himself into his fashions. Beginning in the 1950s, he had his initials monogrammed on most of the outfits in his private wardrobe—including his pajamas. His clothes and jewelry would later feature his personal logo TCB, for "Taking Care of Business." (How many people are cool enough to have their own logo?) When he started studying karate, Elvis's karate master, Kang Rhee, gave him the karate name "Tiger." After that, Elvis incorporated tigers into many of his suits, including as the motif of one of his elaborate stage costumes from the 1970s.

CHAPTER 12
'70S
ACCESSORIES:
BELTS

World's Championship/Attendance Record/Las Vegas Nevada/International Hotel.

—INSCRIPTION ON BELT PRESENTED TO ELVIS ON SEPTEMBER 7, 1970

One of the most eye-catching accessories added to the 1970s costumes were the belts about 4 inches wide. These had huge buckles, 5 to 6 inches high by 7¾ inches wide, and were fit to hang on the hips while riding low in front. Unfortunately, you couldn't have invented a better device if your goal was to draw people's eyes to that little middle-aged paunch.

The most important thing to remember about the belts is that they were completely incorporated into the design of the costume. A studded suit would have a matching studded belt and perhaps a matching cape.

One of the best known of Elvis's belts was one he didn't wear onstage. In 1969, Elvis broke all attendance records during his performance at the International Hotel in Las Vegas. The hotel awarded him a huge belt made of sterling silver overlaid in gold— a kind of wearable trophy. He wore it constantly and you can see it in many interview clips.

The Las Vegas trophy belt is also clearly visible in a famous photograph. Of all the requests made each year to the National Archives for reproductions of photographs and documents, one item has been requested more than any other, more than the Bill of Rights or even the Constitution of the United States. It is the photograph of Elvis Presley and Richard M. Nixon shaking hands on the occasion of Presley's visit to the White House.

ABOVE: THE BELT ... AND THE BLING.
BELOW: ELVIS SPORTING HIS LAS VEGAS TROPHY BELT WHEN MEETING WITH PRESIDENT RICHARD NIXON IN 1970.

I wish they'd make better gold glasses—once you sweat, the gold comes off. The last pair had pink plastic underneath.

—STEVE PERSSON, ETA FROM BELVEDERE, ILLINOIS, QUOTED IN THE *KING AND I* BY KENT BARKER AND KARIN PRITIKIN

Here's how powerful Elvis's image is. Just a pair of his glasses was enough to inspire Czech national Vladimir Lincnovsky to become an Elvis tribute artist. "I brought myself from America one typical souvenir from Graceland," he said. "It was an imitation of Elvis's sunglasses. After that we said that it would be good to do a small Elvis show."

Elvis didn't wear sunglasses to look cool. He wore them for the same reason anyone does—to protect his eyes. Elvis was diagnosed with glaucoma in 1971, which made his eyes extremely sensitive to bright light. Of course, if you're a rock star and you have to wear prescription lenses, you might as well have cool ones.

Elvis's optician, Dennis Roberts, created more than four hundred pairs of sunglasses for The King. The collection was valued at $60,000. The custom frames were frequently emblazoned with the initials EP or the TCB logo. (You've got to wonder, was Elvis afraid of misplacing his stuff?)

The same optician sells reproductions of the glasses, along with "TCB jewelry," mostly on eBay. If you want to be completely authentic, you can go this route—but these items are pricey. It is probably safe to scrimp a bit in this area of your costuming. Elvis-ish glasses can be found many places. There are always lots of them for sale on online auction sites. Blue Suede Films, which produced a documentary on ETAs, sells a $14.95 pair on its Web page. (They're listed in the resource section.)

TIP

BEGINNER'S MISTAKES: ELVIS NEVER WORE HIS SUNGLASSES ONSTAGE. HE WANTED THE FANS TO BE ABLE TO MAKE EYE CONTACT. INSTEAD, HE WORE BROWN CONTACT LENSES TO PROTECT HIS EYES FROM THE GLARE OF THE SPOTLIGHT.

TOP: ELVIS NEVER WORE HIS SUNGLASSES ON STAGE. HOWEVER, THESE IMPERSONATORS HAVE NO PROBLEM WEARING THEM AT A SOCCER MATCH.
BOTTOM: THE ELVIS SHADES MAKE THE MAN.

When you say to an average person "Elvis Impersonator," what they think about is some not terribly great performer all decked out in sequins and sideburns performing at the Best Western off the interstate. And maybe the term "Elvis impersonator" implies a kitsch value that someone performing Elvis circa 1958 doesn't carry. There was nothing kitsch about Elvis on *The Ed Sullivan Show.*

—ROBERT THOMAS, PAST PRESIDENT OF THE INTERNATIONAL POPULAR CULTURE ASSOCIATION

This was the Elvis that changed the world. Young Elvis Aron Presley was the synthesis and the personification of all the musical forces that were bubbling up in postwar America. He didn't invent rock and roll, but he was its most successful ambassador. His look and sound broke down racial barriers, class barriers, and gender barriers. There were a lot of people who had a great deal invested in keeping those barriers intact but, to a generation of youngsters, Elvis represented possibilities, change, and freedom.

Looking back from a new-millennium perspective, it's hard to see just what was so shocking about Elvis's moves. They seem tame compared to anything Britney Spears did when she was still sporting pigtails. But there was something about Elvis—his comfort in his own body, the way he "felt" the music that was indescribably sexy. The idea that your sweet fourteen-year-old daughter might recognize it too … well, that was a bit much for America.

"When you think of Elvis, don't think of the man in the white jumpsuit," says female Elvis Leigh Crow, aka "Elvis Herselvis." "Think of that dangerous boy who was crossing the race barrier, the sex barrier, and scaring all those people. …That's what he was all about."

Who wouldn't want to imitate this personification of rock and roll? But not everyone can. Rockabilly Elvis is a young man's sport. If you're old enough to remember this Elvis, you're too old to play him.

TECHNICAL TIPS: YOU'RE MOST EFFECTIVE IF YOU CAN PERFORM WITH A LIVE BAND WITH A STAND-UP BASS. FOR REAL ICING ON THE CAKE, YOU WANT A CLASSIC '50S-LOOK MICROPHONE, FOR EXAMPLE, THE SHURE MODEL 55SH SERIES II MIC. IT'S ONE OF THOSE GREAT LITTLE DETAILS THAT WILL MAKE YOU SEEM A BIT MORE AUTHENTIC, AND YOUR AUDIENCE MAY NEVER CONSCIOUSLY KNOW WHY. IT GOES WITHOUT SAYING THAT THOSE GARTH BROOKS–MADONNA–BRITNEY HEADPHONE MICS JUST WON'T DO.

TIP

Before you even attempt this Elvis, assess your Elvis strengths. If you get winded walking from your couch to your refrigerator, you're never going to pull it off. If your sense of rhythm leaves something to be desired, steer clear of this Elvis. If you're packing a few extra pounds, perhaps you should look into buying a jumpsuit. Avoid '50s Elvis if you have trick knees and if you can't dance. If you've passed these tests, then you can start working on your early Elvis act.

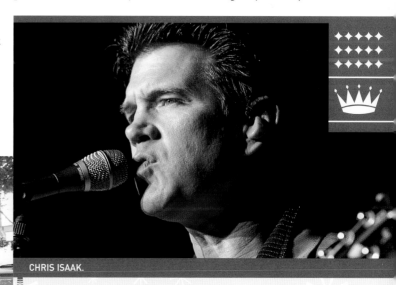

CHRIS ISAAK.

CLOSET ELVIS — CHRIS ISAAK

If he didn't write his own songs and perform in his own TV series, Chris Isaak could do incredibly well on the Elvis tribute artist circuit. He's cultivated the young Elvis look perfectly (although his sound is a bit more Roy Orbison). In 1994, Isaak recorded "Blue Moon" for the Elvis Presley tribute album **It's Now or Never** and performed it on a TV special, backed by guitarist Scotty Moore and drummer D. J. Fontana, former members of Presley's bands. He has also had Lisa Marie Presley as his opening act. When a reporter asked if he was "the Elvis of the '90s," Isaak denied it. "There is no need for an Elvis of the nineties," he said.

ABOVE: TRAVIS LEDOYT ENTERTAINS THE CROWD AT THE ELVIS PRESLEY FESTIVAL IN TUPELO, MISSISSIPPI.

RIGHT: WOLFGANG HAHN OF MEMPHIS, TENNESSEE, IS A COOL '50S ELVIS.

CHAPTER 15
'50S COSTUMES: BEST ELVIS ON A BUDGET

I personally think that Elvis could do his show even in a tracksuit. His fans would certainly let him off with that because of his voice and charisma, two features so adored in Elvis.

—VLADIMIR LINCHOVSKY, "CZECH ELVIS"

ROCKABILLY ELVIS #1 / RYAN PELTON SHOWING OFF HIS ROCKABILLY ELVIS STUFF.

ROCKABILLY ELVIS #2 / ANYTHING THAT EVOKES THE ERA—WITH THE COLLAR UP— WILL WORK FOR ROCKABILLY ELVIS.

ROCKABILLY ELVIS #1

The teenaged Elvis saved up the money he earned as a movie theater usher to buy threads at the Lansky Brothers store on Beale Street in Memphis. That was where much of his 1950s rockabilly gear came from—the Hi-Boy collar shirts, the peg-legged pants, and the suit jackets. (Lansky's is still around, and still selling nostalgic '50s merchandise—look for a listing in the resource section.)

ROCKABILLY ELVIS #2

Elvis's stage clothes were fashionable but not yet showy and costumey. Anything that evokes the era—with the collar up—creates a reasonable impression of Elvis—that is, if you've got the moves down.

JAILHOUSE ROCK ELVIS

The *Jailhouse Rock* costume is easy to put together, and it's instantly Elvis. You just need black slacks, a black-and-white striped shirt, and a black jacket. Note Elvis's dance-scene prison number sewn into the jacket—it's 6240. (Warning: If you can't do the dance—don't put on the costume.) You may also perform this number in a denim jailhouse uniform. This is the one exception to the denim rule below.

TIP

TIP: ELVIS NEVER WORE DENIM, EXCEPT IN HIS MOVIES. JEANS REMINDED HIM OF BEING POOR. UNLESS YOU'RE AN AMAZING LOOK-AND SOUND-ALIKE, DON'T WEAR DENIM FOR YOUR STAGE APPEARANCE. PEOPLE MIGHT THINK YOU'RE TRYING TO BE BOB DYLAN.

WARDROBE MALFUNCTIONS

From his earliest days onstage, Elvis was always splitting his pants. Late in life, people would attribute his torn trousers to his girth, but it was actually his enthusiasm—in the form of dancing—that could not be contained by simple slacks. He sometimes changed right onstage while his band members blocked him from the audience. He told the documentary crew of *Elvis on Tour* that, during his first Vegas appearance, he tore so many costumes that "the audience thought it was part of the show."

TIP: THIS IS A TRICK THAT MANY ACTORS USE BEFORE GOING ONSTAGE. JUST BEFORE YOU STEP ON, CHECK YOUR FLY. SURE, IT SEEMS A LITTLE UNDIGNIFIED, BUT IT IS MUCH MORE DIGNIFIED THAN THE ALTERNATIVE. MORE THAN ONE ELVIS IMPERSONATOR HAS HAD THE UNFORTUNATE EXPERIENCE OF PERFORMING ALL OR MOST OF AN ENERGETIC SET WITH HIS ZIPPER DOWN. DON'T LET THIS HAPPEN TO YOU.

GOLD LAMÉ ELVIS / HONG KONG POP SINGER SAM HUI PERFORMS IN A CLASSIC GOLD LAMÉ SUIT.

TRIVIA QUESTION: IN THE MOVIE *JAILHOUSE ROCK*, ELVIS HAD A DIFFERENT NUMBER ON HIS UNIFORM WHEN HE WAS A PRISONER THAN WHEN HE PERFORMED THE DANCE NUMBER TOWARD THE END. WHAT WAS HIS NUMBER AS A PRISONER?

ANSWER: *6239.*

GOLD LAMÉ ELVIS

Ironically, the 1950s era produced the one costume too gaudy for Elvis. Elvis was blinged out before there was "bling," on the cover of his 1957 album, *50,000,000 Elvis Fans Can't Be Wrong.* The costume was designed by Nudie Cohn, who began his career creating outfits for strippers and showgirls. It was supposed to make Elvis look like a big gold record—get it? Elvis never much liked it; he only wore the full suit, complete with gold slacks and gold shoes, twice in concert. When he slid on his knees in it, he left gold streaks on the stage. But it is now one of the most iconic costumes in rock and roll, and you'd do well to get one yourself if you're doing the '50s. Elvis toned it down by replacing the gold slacks and the frilly silver shirt with plain black.

Whichever '50s look you favor, remember to turn up your collar. Elvis wore his shirt collar up because he was self-conscious of his long neck.

JAILHOUSE ROCK ELVIS / MARIO KOMBOU IN "JAILHOUSE ROCK" AT LONDON'S PICCADILLY THEATER.

CHAPTER 16
'68
"COMEBACK SPECIAL" COSTUMES: TRANSITIONAL ELVIS

There's something magical about watching a man who has lost himself, find his way home. He sang with the kind of power people no longer expect from rock 'n' roll performers.

—JOHN LANDAU, *NEW YORK TIMES*, ON "THE COMEBACK SPECIAL"

ACTOR STACEY WAYNE LOOKING "'68 COMBACK" COOL.

Officially, it was called "Singer Presents Elvis." The world now knows it as "The Comeback Special."

Are you feeling just a bit too old to personify the Hillbilly Cat, but not quite ready to slink into a jumpsuit? This is the Elvis for you—the sleek, sexy leather look of the 1968 television special that reminded America why they'd loved Elvis in the first place.

That said, some segments of this special are highly dated today. They only serve to illustrate how timeless Elvis's early performances were. In the '68 television special, you see groovy modern dancers, go-go lighting, belly dancers, and even a segment with Elvis in what appears to be a brothel full of showgirls in pink hip-huggers. You will not be re-creating any of these (we can only hope).

Instead, focus on the sections with Elvis in leather, especially the low-key pieces—a sort of Elvis Unplugged. In these, Elvis informally jokes with his band and fans, and you get a good sense of his personality.

The all-leather suit that Elvis wore was designed by Bill Belew, who went on to design many of the distinctive Vegas jumpsuits. It was meant to look like a leather version of jeans and a denim jacket. It's about as cool as it gets—also about as hot as it gets. After Elvis had danced to "Heartbreak Hotel," "Hound Dog," and "Jailhouse Rock" under the bright lights, the leather suit literally had to be peeled off his body.

One advantage of the leather suit is that you're unlikely to rip your pants with an ill-executed karate kick. Singer sewing machines were an appropriate sponsor for Elvis, given how frequently he performed that trick. That is one reason he adopted jumpsuits. They gave him more freedom of movement, but he still managed to tear even them.

IF ELVIS JUMPED OFF A BRIDGE ...

Some items from the *Just Because Elvis Did it Doesn't Mean You Should* file:

SING "HOUND DOG" TO A BOXER WHILE WEARING A TUXEDO

SING "OLD MACDONALD" WHILE RIDING ON THE BACK OF A CHICKEN TRUCK

WRITE TO THE PRESIDENT OF THE UNITED STATES AND ASK TO BE MADE AN HONORARY DRUG AGENT

LIE IN BED WATCHING THREE TELEVISIONS AT ONCE

BLAST A HOLE IN YOUR TELEVISION BECAUSE YOU DON'T LIKE THE PROGRAMMING (BUT THEN AGAIN, HAVEN'T WE ALL HAD THIS IMPULSE WHILE WATCHING REALITY TV?)

FRANKIE CASTRO PERFORMS POOLSIDE IN HIS '68 COMEBACK OUTFIT.

CHAPTER 17
MOVIE STAR ELVIS

The only thing worse than watching a bad movie is being in one.

—ELVIS PRESLEY

Although some ETAs say they perform Movie Star Elvis, they really don't. To perform Movie Star Elvis means to perform an Elvis movie and for that you need an entire cast, crew, set, script, dialogue, and production numbers. This is not to say that it's never been done. In fact, *Jailhouse Rock* was recently adapted for the stage and played in London's West End. It was critically panned, but loved by fans, much like Elvis himself.

If you want to make an Elvis movie, get a theatrical agent, audition for Broadway, or try to get financial backing to mount a full-scale theatrical production on your own. You should be aware, of course, that there could be many pitfalls along the way, not the least of which will be getting permission from all the interested parties to use the original music, adapt the script, use the title, and perhaps even use Elvis's image.

In 1999, Danish choreographer Peter Schaufuss created a ballet called *The King*, which told Elvis's life story through dance. It toured Denmark, playing to full houses and standing ovations, but, just days before they were to open in the United Kingdom, Elvis Presley Enterprises got wind of the project and said something to the effect of, "An Elvis ballet? No way." They refused to allow Schaufuss permission to use Elvis's music or to depict the character of Elvis onstage. Schaufuss had to delay his ballet's opening in order to rework the show using lesser-known songs and recordings by other artists. Instead of depicting Elvis, Schaufuss now told the story of "Johnny," an Elvis *impersonator* whose life closely paralleled Elvis's own. The theater offered free seats on the delayed opening night to any costumed Elvis impersonator. Elvis impersonators are better than the searchlights used to advertise car dealerships—they always attract the press.

It is beyond the scope of this book to tell you how to become a theatrical producer or wade through the minefield of permissions; if these are your interests, all we can say is "good luck."

For our purposes, specializing in Movie Star Elvis means doing songs from Elvis's films while dressed in 1950s-style clothes or the Hawaiian gear of *Blue Hawaii*. It doesn't usually mean depicting the

NICHOLAS CAGE, IN *HONEYMOON IN VEGAS*, LOOKING NERVOUS NEXT TO HIS SKYDIVING ELVIS IMPERSONATOR PAL.

film *characters* or full sequences. In the movies, of course, Elvis was not playing Elvis. As an ETA you might enjoy the challenge of playing Elvis playing a sheik, or impersonating Elvis impersonating a cowboy, but your audience probably just won't get it.

There is one notable exception and that is *Jailhouse Rock*. The big production number from that film is instantly recognizable as Elvis, and, if you are able to pull it off, it is an absolute showstopper. Taking on *Jailhouse Rock* is not a beginner's proposition. You need serious stamina to do this highly choreographed film performance. Elvis actually aspirated a cap from one of his teeth while dancing the demanding routine, and had to go to the hospital. Kudos to the performer who can dance the entire number and sing another song afterward.

In any case, you can't ignore Movie Star Elvis. Presley spent a full decade as an actor—longer than any of the other phases of his career.

THE FLYING ELVISES

Are the Flying Elvises from the movie *Honeymoon in Vegas* for real? Well, yes and no. The company of skydiving Elvis impersonators who parachute from the sky with Nicholas Cage in deus ex machina fashion were a fictional creation. What could dramatize the excesses of Las Vegas better than sky-diving Elvises? After the movie came out, people kept calling the production company that developed the film asking how they could book the Flying Elvises. It didn't take long for someone to seize the opportunity: Vegas producer Dick Feeney established a real jumpsuit-and-wig-clad group of divers. He called them the Flying Elvi to avoid any possible trademark disputes with Castle Rock Entertainment. Here's where the story gets interesting. A few Flying Elvi decided to go it alone. They named their group the Flying Elvises and managed to get licensed by Elvis Presley Enterprises. Feeny and his Elvi sued the Elvises and Elvis Presley Enterprises. Graceland agreed to stop working with the Elvises and gave a license to the Flying Elvi instead.

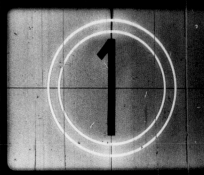

CHAPTER 18
WRITE YOUR OWN ELVIS MOVIE SCRIPT

These are Elvis Presley pictures. They don't need titles. They could be numbered.

—MGM EXECUTIVE QUOTED IN *LOOK* MAGAZINE

Young Elvis Presley dreamed of being a movie star while he worked as a movie usher. He hoped to be a serious thespian in the mold of James Dean or Marlon Brando, and indeed he began his film career with a great deal of promise. His film debut, *Love Me Tender,* was a western, and no time was lost making sure everything was truly authentic to its 1860s time period—none at all. Elvis, as Clint Reno, wears authentic 1866 pomade in his hair as he sings cowboy songs like "We're Gonna Move" to his Southern brothers, who each have Northern accents, while shaking his hips and making the girls squeal. No matter. Anachronisms aside, the young Elvis is quite watchable and showed great potential.

Although Elvis would be offered roles in such quality films as *A Star Is Born, West Side Story, The Defiant Ones,* and *Thunder Road,* his manager, Colonel Parker, turned them all down because he wanted more money. So instead Elvis was directed further and further into lightweight pop movies with forgettable soundtracks and interchangeable plots. For instance, 1967's *Double Trouble* plays like a Monkees episode stretched to a painful two hours—it even featured Monkees regular Monte Landis as the most unlikely guy you'll ever see in a band with Elvis—with musical oddities such as an Elvis Presley rendition of "Old MacDonald." Not even Elvis's star power could save such material.

Elvis knew his place in cinematic history. He once described his own movie career by saying, "One day he's singing to a dog, then to a car, then to a cow. They are all the same damn movie with that Southerner just singing to something different."

Yet he put up with it for a long time, completing thirty-one feature films in all. If you use financial success as your measure, Elvis was probably the biggest movie star of his era.

So, in case you want to personify Movie Star Elvis, we've made it easy for you with this handy guide to create your own Elvis movie script.

Here are the elements you will need. Mix and match:

- An exotic location—Hawaii/Las Vegas/Europe/Acapulco

- Elvis has a dream, often something involving a vehicle—boat race, auto race, buying a fishing boat. …

- But someone does not approve of his dream—his girlfriend/his father/his mother

- You will need two beautiful women. One is vampy and throws herself at Elvis. He will ignore her or rudely reject her. The other is pure and innocent. She will make Elvis chase her. (And sing to her.)

- Although Elvis's character is probably not a professional singer, there must be numerous excuses for him to break into song—he's in love/he enters a singing contest to win money/he gets a part time job in a club/darn it, he's Elvis, he doesn't need a reason.

- At some point Elvis should sing to cute children. (Girls love that.)

- The picture needs a villain—A greedy employer/a romantic rival/a gangster/a cheater trying to beat him in a contest.

- At some point Elvis must get into a fight and punch/karate-chop the villain. Elvis wins the fight. His reasons for the fight may be misunderstood with hilarity ensuing.

- Elvis marries the pure and innocent girl at the end and they both live happily ever after.

- Elvis sings.

SIX DEGREES OF ELVIS

In 1969, Elvis played a character named John Carpenter in the movie *Change of Habit*. In 1979, a real John Carpenter directed an Elvis miniseries for television. The miniseries starred Kurt Russell as Elvis. Kurt Russell made his film debut in 1963 in the Elvis movie *It Happened at the World's Fair*.

SIX DEGREES OF ELVIS 2

James Cann, one of the stars of *Honeymoon in Vegas*, which featured the largest assemblage of Elvis impersonators ever on screen, was married to Sheila Ryan, who had once been romantically linked to the real Elvis Presley. The marriage was on the rocks by the time Cann made *Honeymoon* and found himself in a sea of Elvises. That's gotta hurt.

THINGS YOU SHOULD KNOW ABOUT ELVIS MOVIES

THE NUMBER OF FEATURE FILMS ELVIS MADE: 31

ELVIS'S FIRST FEATURE FILM: *LOVE ME TENDER*

ELVIS'S LAST FEATURE FILM: *CHANGE OF HABIT*

THE OTHER FILM THAT PLAYED AS A DOUBLE BILL WITH *TROUBLE WITH GIRLS: THE GREEN SLIME*

THE ONLY ELVIS FILM IN WHICH ELVIS DOESN'T SING: *CHARRO!*

THE REAL NAME OF "ALBERT," THE GREAT DANE, IN THE FILM *LIVE A LITTLE, LOVE A LITTLE:* BRUTUS (IT WAS ELVIS'S DOG)

THE ONLY SONG BY ANOTHER ARTIST TO BE RELEASED ON AN OFFICIAL ELVIS PRESLEY ALBUM: NANCY SINATRA'S "YOUR GROOVY SELF" FROM THE *SPEEDWAY* SOUNDTRACK

WHO TURNED DOWN THE ROLE OF THE CRUSTY CIRCUS OWNER IN *ROUSTABOUT:* MAE WEST. SHE THOUGHT THE FILM WAS TOO "DOWNBEAT."

WHO TURNED DOWN THE CHANCE TO MAKE *SPEEDWAY* BEFORE ELVIS GOT THE GIG: SONNY AND CHER

THE *L.A. LAW* STAR WHO APPEARED IN *CLAMBAKE:* CORBIN BERNSEN WAS ONE OF THE CHILDREN AT THE PLAYGROUND DURING THE SONG "CONFIDENCE."

THE ONLY FILM SOUNDTRACK FOR WHICH ELVIS DID NOT RECORD ANY NEW SONGS: *TICKLE ME* (ALL THE SONGS HAD BEEN PREVIOUSLY RECORDED BETWEEN 1960 AND 1963)

ELVIS'S MOST SUCCESSFUL FILM IN THEATRICAL RELEASE: *VIVA LAS VEGAS.* IT EARNED $5 MILLION AT THE BOX OFFICE.

THE FILM IN WHICH TERI GARR MADE HER ACTING DEBUT: *FUN IN ACAPULCO* (AS AN UNCREDITED EXTRA)

THE FILM THAT DELAYED ELVIS'S ENTRY INTO THE U.S. ARMY: *KING CREOLE.* HE WAS GIVEN A 60-DAY DEFERMENT TO FINISH THE PICTURE.

THE WORKING TITLE OF *KING CREOLE: A STONE FOR DANNY FISHER*

THE FILM IN WHICH VERNON AND GLADYS PRESLEY MAKE CAMEOS: *LOVING YOU*

THE ONLY ELVIS FILM FOR WHICH ELVIS DID NOT RECEIVE TOP BILLING: *LOVE ME TENDER*

TRIVIA: Elvis's real-life backing musicians, Scotty Moore, Bill Black, and D. J. Fontana, were not allowed to play the roles of the band in Elvis's first movie, *Love Me Tender,* because the casting crew didn't think they looked like country musicians.

CHAPTER 19
GOSPEL ELVIS:
FOR THOSE WITH FAITH

"Nobody was comparing him to Jesus!" I stressed, realizing as I said it that my sin was to have merely talked of Elvis and Jesus in the same breath, the same general frame of reference. Whatever had actually been said, Ellsworth, clearly a pious Christian, had reacted emotionally to the mere proximity of Elvis to Jesus in the discussion.

—WILLIAM McCRANOR HENDERSON, U.S. NOVELIST AND EDUCATOR, *I, ELVIS*

The woman who hires an Elvis impersonator for a bachelorette party is probably not expecting a rendition of "How Great Thou Art," but if you're moved by the spirit and you present it in the right context, you can combine the love of Elvis and the love of Christ to great effect.

One of Elvis's many personas was that of pious gospel singer. As a boy Elvis attended the Assembly of God church and all three of the Grammys Elvis won were for sacred songs.

TRIVIA QUESTION: CAN YOU NAME THE THREE SONGS FOR WHICH ELVIS WON A GRAMMY?

ANSWER: *"How Great Thou Art" (1967), "He Touched Me" (1972), "How Great Thou Art" (1974).*

God-fearing Gospel Elvis is a much overlooked persona in the world of Elvis impersonators but, when it is done, it is done with great gusto.

In addition to sideburns and sequined jumpsuits, Gospel Elvises have sometimes been ordained ministers. Take, for example, James Long, who began his career delivering singing telegrams in Elvis costume and worked his way up the ladder to win the national Elvis competition in Memphis in 1996.

One day, Long was shopping for jewelry that looked like something Elvis might have worn, when he saw a Catholic priest buy a simple cross ring.

"There I was, getting something I really didn't need," Long told the *Chicago Sun-Times,* "and he was completely happy. I wanted to change places."

Shortly thereafter, Long joined the seminary. He still performs Elvis for Catholic fund-raisers from time to time.

Dorian Baxter, of Canada (a much-overlooked hub of Elvis activity), was ordained an Anglican priest on May 15, 1983, by Archbishop Lewis Garnsworthy, St. James Cathedral, Toronto. He was inspired to become a minister, in part, by Elvis's gospel music.

"When I heard Elvis singing gospel music—I think the song that really struck me was 'Without Him I Can Do Nothing.' That is a very powerful song. I knew that this man loved the Lord Jesus Christ with all his heart, mind, soul, and strength."

Soon Baxter was combining his lifelong love of Elvis's music with his religious calling. In an effort to reach the young people in his parish, he rewrote Elvis's lyrics, and formed a band called "Jesus Rock of Our Salvation" to perform them. "Blue Suede Shoes" became "It's one for the father/Two for the son/Three for the Holy spirit/Your life has just begun/You can do anything but don't turn Jesus away."

REVEREND DORIAN BAXTER SINGS DURING A SERVICE AT THE ROYAL CANADIAN LEGION IN NEWMARKET, ONTARIO.

ELVIS AS RELIGION

When speaking to Elvis tribute artists, one is struck by how often references to religion come up.

- "When I die," says Mark Leen, "the first question I'll ask God— and I believe in God, I believe in Jesus Christ, just as Elvis did—the first question I'll ask is 'Where is Elvis?'"

- While some are content to use the music of Elvis to express religious feeling, some see Elvis as a religion in itself.

- Norman J. Giradot, a professor of comparative religions at Lehigh University in Bethlehem, Pennsylvania, created a course, "Jesus, Buddha, Mao, and Elvis," which examines the religion of Elvis. The *Chronicle of Higher Education* reported, "The university has been supportive—although he notes that he didn't introduce the course until after he received tenure. 'It really does touch upon deep and universal aspects of human nature,' he said. 'It's not what you discover about Elvis; it's what you discover about yourself. It's the secret Elvis in all of us.'"

Rumors of his behavior were greatly exaggerated. Baxter says it is completely untrue that he performed funerals in his Elvis jumpsuit and wrote "Return to Sender" on the coffin. Yet something about an Elvis priest didn't sit well with the Anglican authorities, and they asked him to lose the sideburns and cool it with the Elvis thing. Baxter dug in his heels and he is no longer affiliated with the Canadian Anglican Church.

His new independent church is called "Christ the King Graceland."

"The name of our church comes right out of Elvis Presley's mouth," he says. "In 1972, he had the biggest show in the history of Vegas. Colonel Parker had arranged for eighteen of the most beautiful showgirls to come in with flashing letters, and each spelled 'Elvis You Are the King.' This is on video—for people who don't believe me. He got on one knee and he said, 'I thank you for the tribute that you're giving to me. But I'm going to beg you, please don't ever call me "the king" again. He got on one knee and he pointed up to the heavens and he said, 'There is but one king. That is Christ the king.' And we call our church Christ the King Graceland because of the words of Elvis Presley pointing to Jesus."

Of course, you can put the King of Kings into your tribute without starting your own church. You could follow the example Joe Searles, a Virginia-based Elvis impersonator who talks about Elvis's Christian roots and always closes with a gospel song. "I try to put into it the same feeling as if I were sitting down and reading the Bible," he told the *Virginian-Pilot*.

Elvis, incidentally, was also Jewish. Elvis Presley's great-grandfather, White Mansell, married Martha Tackett in 1870. Her mother, Nancy Burdine, was a full-blooded Jew who probably came from a family that emigrated from Lithuania. Under Jewish law, that makes Elvis a Jew. Elvis's mother, Gladys, died in 1959 while Elvis was in the U.S. Army and stationed in Germany. His father bought a headstone bearing a Christian crucifix. Around 1970, Elvis had a Jewish Star of David added to the headstone. In his final years, Elvis wore a necklace with a "chai" pendant (*chai* is the Hebrew word for "living"). He sometimes sported an Egyptian ankh, a Star of David, and a crucifix all at once. He said he didn't want to miss out on Heaven on a technicality.

CHAPTER 20
ELVIS HAIR

If you're like me, and you have your own hair and your own sideburns, and you don't wear wigs people will, as we say in Ireland, slag you. "You ain't nothing but a hound dog," they shout across the street. But that's life, that's the downside of it. The upside is that I have a million euros worth of property that Elvis paid for, and I love my job.

—MARK LEEN, "EMERALD ELVIS"

The first thing that you should know about Elvis's hair is that it was not naturally black. Elvis's naturally sandy brown hair was dyed by his own hand. In the film *Kissin' Cousins,* Elvis played his own twin, a hillbilly "cousin" with dirty blond hair. For those scenes, he had to wear a wig that was similar to his natural hair color. He found the experience quite traumatic. It just wasn't the way he wanted people to see him. According to his costar, Yvonne Craig, he didn't want to come out of the dressing room. To get him on the set, the director had to make everyone promise not to say anything about the wig. The moral of this story is: if your hair is not naturally black, coloration is a must because, without black hair, even Elvis didn't feel like Elvis.

If you love hair grease, then '50s Elvis will be a treat for you to play. Young Elvis was influenced in his grooming by the Southern truck drivers he worked with—a pompadour in front slicked into a DA (duck's ass) in back. It was before the days of hair spray, and the Hillbilly Cat used various types of wax to make his hair do what he wanted—which was mostly to stay put but also to strategically fall. All that "product," as metrosexuals say, is why people who styled their hair like Elvis were known as "greasers."

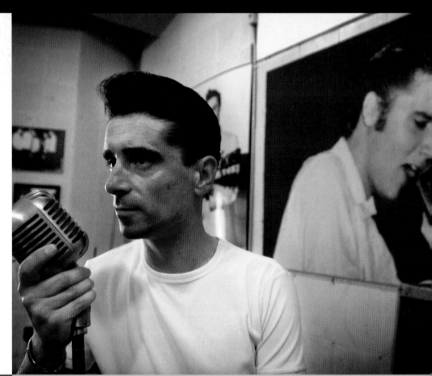

ANTONELLO PERSIANO SPORTS THE PERFECT ELVIS POMPADOUR.

ELVIS HAIR FACTS: Elvis colored his hair with L'Oréal Excellence Blue-Black dye, cleaned it with Wella Balsam shampoo, and styled it with Dixie Peach or Lover's Moon pomade.

Elvis's hair became a bit too perfect in the movies of the 1960s, as studios took control over the Elvis look. The sideburns were gone, and the hair was a beautifully sculpted but uninspiring coif. The real Elvis returned in 1968. During the "Comeback Special," Elvis's hair broke free and fell across his forehead again. Ah, the unruly hair. Welcome back, Elvis!

In the 1970s, Elvis's hair grew longer, sometimes reaching as far as his shoulders. The style was simple and largely overshadowed by the ever-growing sideburns.

DEAN Z. SHOWS OFF HIS '50S POMPADOUR SLICKED INTO A DA.

HOW TO ACHIEVE THE CLASSIC ELVIS POMPADOUR

To achieve this classic look, comb the hair back around the sides of the head. Then use the end of a rattail comb to make a central part at the back of the head. In front, brush the hair upward. Be sure to let a few wayward strands fall down onto your forehead. If your pompadour is too perfect, it ain't Elvis.

BILLIE JOE ARMSTRONG OF GREEN DAY.

CLOSET ELVIS—BILLIE JOE ARMSTRONG

The first record that Billie Joe Armstrong of Greenday ever bought was Elvis Presley's **The Sun Sessions**.

"I remember I wanted to buy an Elvis record," Armstrong recalled, "because I had just seen one of his movies—and he looked the best on the cover of **The Sun Sessions**, so I got that one." The coolest part? "The pompadour!"

TRIVIA: According to *The Guinness Book of World Records,* the most valuable hair clippings ever sold at auction were some black curls that grew out of the head of Elvis Presley. The King's curls were sold by his personal barber, Homer "Gill" Gilleland, for $115,120 on November 15, 2002.

CHAPTER 21
ELVIS
WIGS

We had a guy who was, after a show, with his family in a restaurant, and he looked across a room and saw this sort of worn-out, poor pathetic Elvis impersonator with the big black hair and the big black sideburns. Then he realized it was a mirror and he was looking at himself. He realized at that point, "I can't look like this all the time." I get letters from them after the fact that I changed their life. It's a lot of responsibility.

—ROBERT-CHARLES VALLANCE, BROADWAY WIGS

For maximum authenticity you will want to style your natural hair. But sometimes that just isn't possible. If you perform as GI Elvis and then transition into Aloha Elvis for your second act, you can't grow out your hair during the intermission. One of those hairstyles will have to be faked.

You may also be a bit follicularly challenged. If your hairline has receded, or you need some patching in the back, you might go with a wig. You can also contact a provider of hair replacements, such as Hair Club, and tell them about your unique needs. They can create hairpieces for you that give you an Elvis look.

Wigs can also save your career. Your *other* career, that is. If you're a doctor by day, you might not instill confidence if you have Elvis hair. Elvis was many things, but a surgeon he was not.

The trick is to get a wig that doesn't look like the hound dog has died on your head. The Elvis wigs you get from Halloween costume shops are a one-size-fits-none proposition. Quality theatrical wigs are different. Each individual strand of hair—either the real human stuff, or a synthetic material—is hand-tied to a cap of lace netting that virtually disappears under stage lighting. It's also made upon a head mold, so the fit is precise.

How is a head mold made? I'm glad you asked. It's a low-tech operation that you will probably want to carry out in private. The tools you will need are clear plastic wrap, clear cellophane tape, and a black marker. You can download detailed instructions from the Web page **www.broadwaywigs.com**, but the short version is, you wrap your head in the plastic, reinforce it with the tape, and trace your hairline with the marker—the hairline you really have, not the one you wish you had. (Caution: Apparently some folks get a bit overzealous in their taping and they can't get the mold off.) Once you have your mold, send it off to a professional wig maker with a description of the hair you want.

"Some of our guys are very specific," says Robert-Charles Vallance, a wig maker for Broadway and film who has made wigs for about four hundred Elvises. "They want frame number 280 from the '68

Comeback Special,' where the hair falls right in the front with the bead of sweat. Okay, guys, you have to supply your own bead of sweat."

Wigs of this quality do not come cheap. A good one will run anywhere from $750 to $3,000—a small price to pay for something that lets you be Elvis while keeping your day job.

"I had two guys fly into New York with their bed rolls and their jumpsuits," Vallance said. "They had not arranged hotel rooms. They walked around the city for three days because they weren't going to pay that kind of money for a hotel room, but they would pay that kind of money for a wig."

MICHAEL LEVICK CARING FOR HIS ELVIS WIG.

Fun is fun, but swooning over someone who looks a lot like Elvis but also looks a lot like Union Army Gen. Ambrose Burnside strikes me as, well, having a bit too much fun.

—BOB ALLEN, *CRAIN'S DETROIT BUSINESS*

Sideburns. Any Elvis tribute artist worth his salt grows his own (unless he is too young or female to do so). Growing mutton chops, however, represents a certain level of commitment. You have to be willing to be heckled in the grocery store. It means having a day job that allows for a relaxed dress code (not recommended for corporate executives).

Of course, there are other reasons to keep your natural sideburns cropped. Some performers use fakes because, like Craig Newell, of Nevada, they perform Elvises of different periods. Newell uses high-quality theatrical sideburns made by the same wig maker that supplies NBC's *Saturday Night Live*. This way, he can use his natural sideburns for early Elvis and paste on the biggies for Vegas Elvis.

The key to repeated wear of fake sideburns is quality. Quality faux sideburns are available from theatrical wig makers and they run from $150 to $200, depending on the style. The sideburns last for about two years when well cared for. It's important to clean off the adhesive well after every performance. Buildup of adhesive breaks down the fibers.

Of course, you want to be sure they stay on your face. You can buy sweat inhibitor, i.e., facial antiperspirant, at stores that sell theatrical supplies. The stuff you use under your arms would probably work but, if you go that route, be sure you get a separate container for that purpose, for obvious sanitary reasons. Put the inhibitor around the edge of the burn to keep it from being washed off when you sweat. Nothing will turn a tribute into a parody faster than a sideburn that is wiggling more than your legs.

TIP: IF YOU HAVE A TOUCH OF GRAY IN THE BURNS, YOU CAN DO TOUCHUPS WITH A LITTLE MASCARA BEFORE YOU GO ONSTAGE. IT'S NOT CHEATING, THE KING DID IT HIMSELF.

TIP

SIDEBURN MALFUNCTION 1:
In the 2005 television mini-series *Elvis* starring Jonathan Rhys-Meyers, the glue and makeup on Elvis's sideburns is clearly visible during close-ups in a scene where he discusses being drafted with his parents and Col. Tom.

SIDEBURN MALFUNCTION 2:
Matt King, a Michigan-based ETA, told the authors of *Walk a Mile in Their Shoes:* "I was onstage performing and one of the fans in the front row yelled, 'Hey, Matt! Be careful you're stepping on something!' At that point I looked down and saw my left sideburn stuck to my foot. A week later, I grew my own real ones."

43

CHAPTER 23
SING LIKE THE KING

Learning to be Elvis is no different than learning to be a singer. It's just a little more specific.

—BRIAN SIMPSON, CANADA-BASED ELVIS

The comedian Billy Crystal, as Fernando, popularized the saying, "It's better to look good than to feel good." When it comes to impersonating Elvis, however, the right sound is crucial. Ideally, you want to have the look and the sound, but if you can only master one—go with the voice.

If people hear Elvis when they close their eyes, you can get away without any costume at all, but even the best costuming in the world will fail to win you fans if your singing voice is more like that of Tiny Tim than of Elvis Presley.

Kavee Thongprecha is an insider's hit with his weekend Elvis performances at the Palms Thai Restaurant, in Hollywood. He doesn't have the flashy costumes but he sounds a lot like Elvis, and hearing that voice come out of someone who looks so unlike The King is what keeps people coming back.

Steve Chappell is another Elvis with no resemblance whatsoever to Presley. He foregoes the sideburns and keeps his own curly brown hair as God made it. He has an impish grin with not a trace of Elvis lip curl, yet he's been successfully performing Elvis songs and moves for a decade.

So here are a few tips on mastering the Elvis vocal style:

- Elvis was a musical sponge. In addition to his obvious blues, country, and gospel influences, Elvis Presley admired the opera singer Mario Lanza and tried to sing like him. Although Elvis was an untrained singer, he had a three-octave vocal range and could reach the C above the middle C. You may need a few singing lessons to emulate this.

- Doug Church has created an instructional DVD complete with lessons on breath control, vocal warm-ups, and tips on posture. What makes his singing lesson different than others is that Church is known as "The Voice of Elvis," and in the DVD he explains how to emulate Elvis's vibrato and phrasing. The DVD, *Sing like the King,* is available from Blue Suede Films, the company that found a niche in the ETA market after creating the documentary *Almost Elvis* (see resource section).

ETA DON ROSE SINGS HIS HEART OUT LIKE THE KING.

• If you don't want to spring for *Sing like the King,* any musical training can give you the basics. For inexpensive musical instruction, try auditioning for your church choir and practice, practice, practice. Elvis Presley got his start this way. He sang in the choir at the First Assembly of God Church, in Tupelo, Mississippi, and it was here that he gave his first public performances as a singer. In fact, his earliest musical influences may have been the pastors who played guitar along with church services.

• Once you get down the basics, you can start working on those distinctive Elvis-isms, particularly his vibrato. Get out some records and listen to what Elvis does. The vibrato is easy to overdo. "Elvis didn't have vibrato throughout the song; if he did, he'd sound like Katherine Hepburn," Doug Church observes. "If your vibrato is not consistent and it's not authentic, then you're better off not using it at all."

• Another beginner's mistake is to slur words together. Elvis had a Southern accent, but he was not sloppy in his singing. You can always tell what he is saying. Imitators tend to let the words trail off or make an entire line into one long, indistinct word.

• Barbara Del Piano, aka Belvis, is a female Elvis tribute artist who sounds like The King in a weird "that's biologically impossible" sort of way. In her normal feminine speaking voice, she says: "The key to sounding like Elvis is to really listen to him. Some of the people that I've heard do Elvis don't sound like him. You have to really listen to the man. Don't do his persona. Do what he sounds like. The persona is hum-hum-baby-hey-baby-hunka-hunka. I've heard some performers do that ho-huh-baby-ho-huh and it's not him. If you're going to put on that jumpsuit, you'd better sound like him. You'd better have respect for the jumpsuit if you're going to put it on. If you don't sound like him, hang up the jumpsuit—with respect."

MARK LEEN, EMERALD ELVIS, PAYS TRIBUTE IN SONG.

CHAPTER 24
SELECT YOUR
SIGNATURE
SONG

There are some songs that Elvis did that personally I wouldn't want to learn. Like "Old Shep." I've had to put my dog down, and it just isn't a song I really want to learn.

—DON OBUSEK, PITTSBURGH-BASED ELVIS

With 739 officially released Elvis songs to choose from, you're probably safe leaving movie gems "There's No Room to Rhumba in a Sports Car" and "Yoga Is as Yoga Does" off your set list. "Harem Holiday," "Queenie Wahine's Papaya" and "Song of the Shrimp" are probably safe to avoid as well. Some of the most questionable Elvis movie songs—think "Do the Clam"—were co-written by Dolores Fuller, the ex-wife of B-movie director Ed Wood. A good rule of thumb is, if it came from an Elvis movie made after 1960, think twice.

The year 1960 is just a guideline. The later films did spawn a few gems, such as "A Little Less Conversation," which was written for the 1968 movie *Live a Little, Love a Little*. It was remixed and in 2002 became a hit in the United Kingdom, and was even adopted as the theme song of the British Conservative Party in the last election.

Then there are the songs that you may save for special occasions because of the toll they can take. "Burning Love" is so hard to sing that even Elvis dropped it from his live performances, likewise "Viva Las Vegas."

But that's what not to do. What should you do? The important thing when assembling a set list is pacing. "You want to pick 'em up, carry 'em along and drop 'em off wanting more," says Todd Martin, a Louisiana-based ETA.

If you're doing a late-period Elvis, you can take a cue from his own set list. Before you come onstage, let the excitement build by playing "Also Sprach Zarathustra" (aka the theme from *2001: A Space Odyssey)*. Be advised that such a dramatic opening produces certain expectations. Be prepared to wow them with your entrance. Segue into "See See Rider," The King's traditional opening from this era. From there, go into another fast song without stopping, before moving into a ballad. Keep the mood flowing, and be aware of your own energy level. Bring the audience back up before finishing your show. Elvis always closed with "Can't Help Falling in Love with You." Most tributes do, too. And don't forget the end theme—Da da DAH! You can find it on a number of 1970s-era live recordings. C'mon, admit it, don't you wish you had your own theme music?

SONG ADVICE FROM AN EXPERT

"Elvis did many songs by other entertainers, like 'Unchained Melody.' 'You've Lost that Loving Feeling,' and 'Yesterday,'" says Pittsburgh Elvis impersonator Don Obusek. "If you throw some of those other songs in with the hard core, you're not only touching the hard-core Elvis people, you're getting people saying, 'I never knew he did that, that's pretty cool,' and they tend to come around. They're into the show because they like these other entertainers— Neil Diamond or the Beatles or whoever— and you're drawing in the rest of the crowd."

BELOW: PETE SEEGER.

CLOSET ELVIS—PETE SEEGER

The folk singer Arlo Guthrie often tells the story of a folk festival in Denmark, shortly after the Berlin Wall came down. The small festival grew to an event with 30,000 people from eastern and western Europe able to celebrate together for the first time. Arlo was performing with folk legend Pete Seeger. Seeger had just led the crowd through the most world-famous folk songs, "We Shall Overcome" and the like. Then he turned to Arlo Guthrie and asked him to sing something. Arlo realized that Pete had already sung all the songs that Arlo thought anybody might know.

Arlo didn't know what to do, so he said, "Well, here's one you might know. Made popular by that king of folksingers ... Elvis Presley. Pete looked at me. ... We'd been singing them peace and love songs for decades, but folk singers would argue themselves to death over what a folk song was."

Arlo played the first verse. "I got just that far through the song and I realized that there was 30,000 people singing along with me. Every one of them knew the words. So Pete looked at **them,** and I was feeling safer. Then Pete got up and walked up to the micro-phone. I didn't know what he was going to say. He didn't say nothing. He just started playing it on the banjo. That's when I realized that Pete knew it too. ... Here we were singing an old Elvis tune that didn't have much to say about the state of the world but more was being said by who was singin' it and how they were feelin' than trying to sing songs that try to say a whole lot of stuff."

> I'm not kidding myself. My voice alone is just an ordinary voice. What people come to see is how I use it. If I stand still while I'm singing, I'm dead, man. I might as well go back to driving a truck.
>
> —ELVIS PRESLEY

CHAPTER 25
MOVES

Before you start looking at any specific moves, you need to put yourself in the right frame of mind. Imagine that there is an electric force inside you that is just trying to get out. It takes all your energy to rein it in. Eventually, it has to escape. First, your leg jiggles just a bit, then more, and next thing you know it breaks loose entirely. Dance as if your body responds to the music without any will of your own and in spite of your best efforts to control it.

For your dance education, you can watch some of Elvis's contemporaries as well. You can safely crimp a few moves from such folks as Chubby Checker. Watch him do the slow twist and you'll see a move that Elvis performed as well. Just don't try to copy most of the white guys who were around at the same time as Elvis. As a point of comparison watch the Dovells doing the Bristol Stomp. Golly.

Once you get the feel of moving like a rockabilly idol or a Vegas-era King, embrace it, and forget trying to copy everything you see.

"In terms of dancing, he was just doing what he felt out there," says Travis LeDoyt, "and you just kind of do the same. Feel the music and move to it. If you think about it, it will look fake. You're not getting any closer to him by doing the exact moves. If you want to get closer to him—to what he was feeling—you've got to wing it. Put yourself out there and be in the moment."

CHAPTER 26
'50S (MOVIE) MOVES

To begin doing the classic Elvis Presley moves, be sure you start with the proper stance. You should position yourself with your feet slightly wider than shoulder width apart. Your feet should be turned slightly outward; this allows for quick changes of motion in any direction. Your weight should be on the balls of your feet.

TILT-IN KNEES—To execute the most basic and recognizable Elvis move, swivel your hips and shift your weight so that one knee can quickly bend inward and snap back, then repeat with the opposite leg, on the beat of the music, of course.

THE TIP-TOE CHAIR—Bend at the waist as though you were sitting in an invisible chair, and at the same time raise your weight onto the tops of your toes.

THE EXAGGERATED RUN—This is nothing more than a stylish jiggly run in place with exaggerated knee bends, putting the weight on the balls of your feet then snapping back onto the soles.

THE SLOW TWIST—One of Elvis's favorite movie moves is the slow twist, with arms bent at the waist and fingers snapping, he swivels his hips with his legs relaxed and apart.

THE ROCK—Raise your feet so that you're balanced on the tips of your toes and bend your knees while remaining upright. The microphone stand can be used for balance.

THE ROLL—Next comes the stuff that made the girlies squeal and the censors cringe. Moved by the spirit, the pelvis and the whole torso are brought into the movement. Feet apart the hips move right and left and even forward and back.

TILT-IN KNEES.

TRIVIA QUESTION: TALK ABOUT INTIMIDATION— WHILE ELVIS WAS PERFORMING THE "JAILHOUSE ROCK" MOVES FOR THE FILM OF THE SAME NAME, A FAMOUS HOOFER WAS WATCHING. CAN YOU NAME HIM?

ANSWER: *Gene Kelly.*

Above all, respect your own body's capabilities. "When you're jogging around the stage trying hard to imitate every single Elvis movement, it usually ends up being funny instead of being sexy and interesting," says Czech Elvis impersonator Vladimir Lichnovsky.

THE ROCK.

CHAPTER 27

'70S MOVES

Doing the karate splits ... I once lost my balance and landed on my pride.

—ART KISTLER, ETA QUOTED IN *WALK A MILE IN THEIR SHOES*

In the 1970s, Elvis left more time between the fancy moves. There was more pacing of the stage, more pauses but, when he did move, the poses were dramatic.

THE NERVOUS LEG—While standing still, allow one leg to start twitching as if it were itching like a man on a fuzzy tree. All Shook Up—Eventually the above leg movement gives way to an all-out body shake. Every limb quivers.

THE LOWERED TRIPOD—Bend the left knee while extending the right knee out straight. This is similar to a warm-up stretch for running.

THE ARM SWING—Keeping your body relatively stiff, swing one arm back and forth as if you're trying to throw it away. This is good for highly dramatic songs. After a few songs, you can raise the same arm above your head as if you were trying to stop traffic. Leave your hand up as you sing an extended long note.

KARATE KICK—You can get this from studying videos of Elvis or karate champions. Raise your leg quickly and extend it fully as if you're knocking over an opponent. A black belt in karate helps to execute this move, but it is optional. (If you learn the move from Bruce Lee, be sure to omit the screams.) This move requires some skill and is one of the most likely to result in injury if not executed correctly.

KARATE KICK.

BEGINNER'S MISTAKES: AMATEUR ELVISES TEND TO OVERDO THE MOVES. THE REAL ELVIS WAS NOT CONSTANTLY IN MOTION. THE "ELVIS-Y" MOVES ARE LIKE TABASCO SAUCE. A LITTLE BIT IS A SPICY TREAT. TOO MUCH RUINS THE WHOLE DISH. NOT ONLY IS CONSTANT FLAILING INAUTHENTIC, YOU WILL WEAR YOURSELF OUT BY THE SECOND SONG.

TIP

THE GUITAR TOSS—At the end of the song, remove the guitar and casually toss it offstage (only do this if you have someone there to catch it). The key to this move is, under no circumstances should you turn to see if your friend catches it. Be sure you let your backstage accomplice know the musical cue for the toss or you'll be investing in a lot of guitar repair.

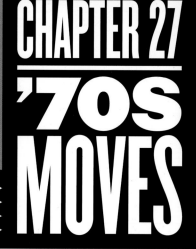

THE LOWERED TRIPOD.

CHAPTER 28
STAGE PRESENCE

That's my idol, Elvis Presley. If you went to my house, you'd see pictures all over of Elvis. He's just the greatest entertainer that ever lived. And I think it's because he had such presence. When Elvis walked into a room, Elvis Presley was in the f-ing room. I don't give a f- who was in the room with him, Bogart, Marilyn Monroe.

—EDDIE MURPHY

JOHNNY THOMPSON TAKES IN THE AUDIENCE AT "A WEEKEND WITH THE KING" IN MAY 2003.

STAGE PRESENCE IS ALL ABOUT ENJOYING YOURSELF AND CONVEYING THAT JOY TO THE AUDIENCE.

Now that you look the part, it's time to start working on your performance.

As you go through the process of releasing your inner Elvis you will find that some things come more naturally to you than others. You may be an Elvis look-alike with no sense of rhythm. Perhaps you are shorter, taller, heavier, or more Asian than the real McCoy. Maybe you have the moves down but your singing leaves something to be desired.

Whatever your weakness is—don't worry, you can get away with it as long as you play up your strengths. The only ingredients that you can't do without are charisma and a sense of humor. That's a pretty good guide to life as well.

There is no magic formula, but here is what the experts have to say on the subject of commanding the stage. To quote a song from the movie *Clambake,* "There's no job too immense when you've got confidence."

TRAVIS LEDOYT: I'm imitating him, but I'm not copying. I'm not doing every finger movement he did and every leg movement, but I'm doing the same style. It is an impersonation of Elvis. It's not a re-creation exactly of a show, it's what a show probably could look like. You try to make it a new show of Elvis's. If you only did exactly what you saw, it would get dull to yourself and to the fans. So you

have to put a little bit of yourself into it a little of your own humor as long as it's authentic to the times.

PAUL HYU: It is down to the performer to make the audience enjoy themselves. The more they are enjoying themselves, the more they will forgive you and the more you can stray from trying to "be" Elvis.

JOHN LOOS: I've seen tribute artists who are exactly like Elvis. They do everything like Elvis. It gets kind of boring; it's like watching a robot onstage—if anything ever happens that's not in the video, they don't know what to do.

TODD MARTIN: There are a lot of good singers out there, but Elvis had the "it," but nobody knows what the "it" is. ... You don't have to look like Elvis. It's all acting and mannerisms.

CLOSET ELVIS— BORIS YELTSIN

In 1991 after standing on a tank in Moscow to rally democratic forces against a fascist coup, Yeltsin returned alone to his office to listen to Elvis Presley's "Are You Lonesome Tonight?"

RUSSIAN PRESIDENT BORIS YELTSIN DOING THE TWIST.

Is being Elvis like method acting?

—ACTOR HARVEY KEITEL TO ELVIS IMPERSONATOR RICK MARINO ON THE SET OF *FINDING GRACELAND*, 1988

ETA, MIKE ALBERT, CROONING TO A FAN.

Don't let your Elvis down between songs. The best ETAs practice such minutiae as how Elvis drank his water—with his hand facing his body as he tipped the glass. Before you get onstage, be sure you put in at least a little time practicing walking and talking like Elvis. Nothing blows the illusion like ending a rousing "Jailhouse Rock" and then standing uncomfortably as you say, "Yeah, um, well, perhaps you'd like to hear, you know, this one called 'Love Me Tender'?"

If you're from a Southern state, you should not have trouble with it. If, on the other hand, you're from New York, Boston or Fargo, it might be a little jarring if you use your own accent between songs. It will take you further still from the illusion of Elvis if you open your mouth and your dialect is from Glasgow, Johannesburg, or Sydney.

Jonathan Rhys-Meyers, who played Elvis in the recent CBS miniseries, is an Irishman. He worked with a dialect coach and had all of his dialogue written out in phonetics. You won't have to do as much speaking as he did, and your dialogue will probably be improvised, which means this method of study might not be as practical.

It is difficult to write about accents without using phonetics and linguistic diagrams, so the best advice we can give you is to rent a few Elvis movies and imitate the way he talks. Just to get you started, here is a description of Elvis's regional accent, from a theatrical dialogue coach, Neill Hartley, adjunct assistant professor at the University of the Arts, in Philadelphia:

> "Elvis Presley had a sound that was placed toward the back of his mouth somewhat," Hartley says. "It's interesting because a lot of the South, what I'll call the Deep South, has a placement that is lighter—toward the front of the mouth—but his seems to be back a bit. It can be common with some folks, especially African-American people from Mississippi down into Louisiana. And he has very typical characteristics of the Deep South, and especially the rural Deep South."

51

Well spotted. The Presleys moved a great deal when Elvis was a boy, and Elvis would have picked up speech patterns from a number of different neighbors. By the time he entered the seventh grade the Presley family was living in what has been described as "a house designated for whites—only in a respectable colored neighborhood."

His speech characteristics include shifts in the vowel sounds (from Northern speech). Southerners tend to draw out and add an extra sound (a diphthong) to certain vowels, yet with the "i" and the "oi" sound they truncate it, cutting the diphthong in half, so the word "I'm" pronounced up north as "I-ee-m" is more like "Ah-m" in Mississippi.

By the 1970s, Elvis's speech would have been influenced ever so slightly by his time in the army, his years in Hollywood, and all the diverse people he spent time with. If you specialize in a later-period Elvis, you should listen to tapes of his speech from that era.

Doug Church, a native of Michigan, in his instructional video *Sing like the King,* talks about the challenge of sounding like Elvis.

"Elvis was relaxed," he says, "but he also, at one point, sounded like a Southerner trying not to sound like a Southerner, so here you are, a Northerner, trying to sound like a Southerner trying to sound like a Northerner. It's like Victor-Victoria."

If you're looking for samples of Elvis's speech, you might pick up a copy of the boxed set *Elvis Live in Las Vegas.* It has lots of extended stage patter, and it demonstrates that, even in the 1970s, Elvis hadn't lost his Southern accent.

Of course, no matter what you do, you're not going to sound *exactly* like Elvis, because his bone structure was unique.

"Speech can also vary depending on the actual instrument," Hartley says. "Elvis was male. He had a certain physicality. The shapes of the cavities inside his body—his mouth, the back of the mouth, the nose—all of that affects speech and how it vibrates in the body. That is why no two people sound exactly alike."

CHAPTER 30
THE LIP CURL

Byron [the great English Romantic poet] and Elvis Presley look alike, especially in strong-nosed Greek profile. In Glenarvon, a roman à clef about her affair with Byron, Caroline Lamb says of her heroine's first glimpse of him, "The proud curl of the upper lip expressed haughtiness and bitter contempt." Presley's sneer was so emblematic that he joked about it. In a 1968 television special, he twitched his mouth and murmured, to audience laughter, "I've got something on my lip." The Romantic curling lip is aristocratic disdain. ... Byron and Presley had early and late styles: brooding menace, then urbane magnanimity. Their everyday manners were manly and gentle. Presley had a captivating soft-spoken charm. ... Byron and Presley were world-shapers, conduits of titanic force, yet they were deeply emotional and sentimental in a feminine sense.

—CAMILLE PAGLIA, *SEXUAL PERSONAE*

Elvis could make women swoon with the smallest movement of his levator labii superioris. That's the muscle between the nose and the upper lip. ... What did you think it was?

One of the misconceptions about Elvis's trademark lip curl was that it was a sneer of aggression. Careful observation will reveal that the lip thing was just Elvis's smile. It usually rears its head when Elvis snickers at the reactions of his female fans to his gyrations. Curling your lip into a snarl is more Billy Idol than Elvis.

As it happens, Elvis was quite gifted in the lip-curling department.

Although he was primarily left-lipped, he could go both ways. Most people can only sneer on one side or the other. Deborah Targoff, at the Classen School of Advanced Studies, did a study on sneering ability by observing 138 individuals. Of her sample, 35 percent could only sneer on the right, 41 percent only on the left, and 12 percent couldn't do it at all. Only 12 percent were ambi-lip-curlous like Elvis.

If you can't curl your lip at all, there is probably not much you can do about it. You can try exercising your upper lip, but there is no guarantee that this will produce results. You're better off perfecting some other Elvis trait to compensate.

RIGHT: THE ELVIS LIP CURL CAN SOMETIMES TURN INTO A SNARL.

BELOW: LORD BYRON THE ENGLISH ROMANTIC POET AND ELVIS LOOK ALIKE, REPRESENTING EARLY AND LATE STYLES: BROODING MENACE, THEN URBANE MAGNAMITY.

CLOSET ELVIS — BILLY IDOL

During his college years in England, Billy Idol worked nights as a postal worker: "One night I was singing to myself 'Don't Be Cruel,' by Elvis Presley," he once said, "and a bloke said the classic, 'Don't ever try singing for a living.'" Billy Idol rejected his advice, and sneered his way into MTV fame.

BILLY IDOL.

53

CHAPTER 31
YOUR ENTOURAGE

Losing a twin brother at birth equally affected Elvis. Many identical twins believe they are 'half' of the other twin, or half of a person. ... If one twin dies at birth, the other often feels abandoned and alone or dependent upon having people around him until he or she dies. ... In later life, Elvis kept an entourage of people with him at all times. ...

—PATRICIA JOBE PIERCE, *THE ULTIMATE ELVIS*

Elvis Presley was the second born of a set of twins. Whether Elvis and his stillborn brother, Jesse Garon Presley, were identical or fraternal is not known, but most authorities opt for identical. There is always a hint of "what could have been" surrounding Elvis, and the idea of a pair of identical Presley boys fits well into the mythology.

Those who are fond of psychoanalyzing celebrities like to attribute Elvis's constant need for company to the loss of his twin. Whether you buy the explanation or not, it is a fact that Elvis was rarely alone.

One of the most notable things about Elvis Presley's performances was the close friendship he seemed to have with the members of his band and crew. He was always joking with them, and he relied on them to hand him his scarves and water and to keep the show moving along. In his private life, Elvis was surrounded by friends and supporters known as "the Memphis Mafia."

A solitary Elvis with recorded music is already well removed from the picture we have of the real Elvis. The solution? Get yourself your own Memphis Mafia. You need some tough-looking bodyguards to usher you to and from the stage. They can hand you your scarves and untangle your guitar cords as well.

Early on, you may have a friend or two who will do this for fun, but don't expect them to keep it up unless you're able to pay them. It's only fair. Professional entertainers often have a support crew—sound men, road managers, and so on. When you get to the point that you need a support staff of your own, get them some "Elvis" jackets and be sure you hire folks who are willing to do a little acting.

PRENTICE CHAFFIN POSES WITH AN ENTOURAGE.

WHO FIRST SAID, "ELVIS HAS LEFT THE BUILDING"?

It was Horace Lee Logan, founder of the country radio show *Louisiana Hayride*, where Elvis got his big break in 1954. Logan's instincts had been right on when he signed the young unknown to a regular performing contract. Next thing you know, Elvis was a national sensation. Elvis bought out his contract for $10,000 (a huge sum in those days) but agreed to perform one last time on the *Hayride*, on December 15, 1956. Teenagers packed the studio screaming with such abandon that it was hard to even hear their idol. Elvis was not the only performer scheduled that day, but after he left the stage, the kids just wouldn't stop shouting for him. That's when Logan got onstage and tried to calm Elvis's fans. "Please, young people," he said, "Elvis has left the building. He has gotten in his car and driven away. Please take your seats."

The expression didn't become a staple of Elvis concerts until 1971. At the Cleveland Public Hall Auditorium, Al Dvorin, a former bandleader and long-time concessionaire, took over as announcer. It was he who institutionalized the phrase at the end of each show.

Interviewer: Your actions make quite a reaction in the audience. What's your opinion of the audience?

Elvis Presley: Well, I mean it would look pretty funny out there without one.

It is not an Elvis show unless women are crying and screaming. You can even plant one or two fainters in the crowd. For the most part, however, you won't need to make any arrangements. People who come to see an Elvis impersonator expect to play along.

"It's like I tell the audience," says Todd Martin, "I'm up here and I'm acting. I'm acting like Elvis. You need to act, too, and we'll all have a good time. The more they get into it, the more I do."

In case you're wondering, Elvis tribute artists do have fans of their own. They have fan clubs and people who travel long distances to see their favorites. With an impersonator, they can have more time and personal contact then they could ever have had with Elvis Presley.

"We have a little fan club and we have parties at my house and parties at a restaurant," says Todd Martin. "I've always said that if you were a fan of Tim McGraw or somebody, you're not going to get to be a part of anything—be around him and go do stuff. We're just like family and friends."

There are even rumored to be Elvis tribute groupies—gals who want to bed as many Elvises as they can. They are known as "sideburn chasers."

Here are a few tips for female audience members on how you can participate in the show:

- When "Elvis" enters the building, put your hands on the side of your face, jump up and down, and scream. For added dramatic effect, you can grab the sides of your hair, or shake it uncontrollably.

- If you're watching a 1950s Elvis, don't forget to titter and squeal at the "naughty" movements, i.e., whenever your Elvis shakes his pelvis.

- If you're planning to see a 1970s Elvis, be sure to pack some white handkerchiefs, which you can hand up to him when he starts to glisten. (Hint: You may want to keep a zip-top plastic bag in your purse to keep the contents clean when you get the sweaty version back.)

- You get bonus points as an audience member if you can make your eyes well with tears when "Elvis" sings a slow love song.

They may not give out awards for the best audience-member tribute performance, but you will know when you get it right, and you can take pride in performing a valuable service to the ETA onstage.

STEVE HARWELL.

CLOSET ELVIS—
SMASH MOUTH'S STEVE HARWELL

"I've been picking up Elvis stuff on tour," Steve Harwell of Smash Mouth once said. "I'm into Elvis Presley big time. I just got a Young Elvis phone. He has a guitar on and when it rings he sings 'Jailhouse Rock' and dances. Our keyboard player bought it at a Flying J truck stop for me. I woke up and it was in my bunk lying next to me. It's, like, a foot high. So, yeah, I slept with Elvis. We spooned."

CHAPTER 33

35,000 ELVIS IMPERSONATORS CAN'T BE WRONG, OR BEING ELVIS WHILE BEING YOURSELF

The "spirit of Elvis"—if that is the essence of what an ETA is trying to achieve—has in fact very little to do with vocal stylings, dress sense, hair, and accessories, but more to do perhaps with respectfulness, innovation, and race relations.

—PAUL HYU, "CHINESEELVIS"

You can aspire to Elvisness without losing your unique personality. And with an estimated 35,000 Elvis impersonators out there, it pays to have a gimmick. Elvisness is not for whites only, not for men only, not for Americans only. The image of Elvis is big enough to include us all.

Barbara Del Piano, aka "Belvis," had a couple of extra considerations when selecting her '70s-era Elvis jumpsuit.

"The jumpsuit zippers only go so far," she says. "They're cut low for a man. My tailor has been working that out for me. I've been zipping them up as high as they go, and I've had some clips put in to cover. I put my scarf inside to cover that up and I go into character. "I'm in no way Britney Spears. I don't go out with the cleavage hanging out."

Belvis is what you might call an alternative Elvis, a type of which form a group of performers that includes African Americans, Latinos, Asian Americans, the disabled, and foreign nationals. They were not born with the obvious look of Elvis and so they have to work a bit harder to create the illusion—but there is no shortage of nonwhite male pretenders to the Elvis throne. In fact, some of the best Elvises in the business are nonwhite. Robert Washington of Maine, an African American, was the 2003 winner of the "Images of the King" Contest in Memphis—the "Good Housekeeping Seal of Approval" of the Elvis tribute world.

After all, Elvis himself is often said to have been an "impersonator" of black music. "The colored folks been singing and playing it just like I'm doing now, man, for more years than I know," Elvis once said. "I got it from them. … I used to hear Arthur Curdup bang his box the way I do now, and I said if I ever got to the place where I could feel all old Arthur felt, I'd be a music man like nobody ever saw."

That's not to say that nontraditional Elvises always have an easy time of it.

"People expecting a 'Tribute to Elvis' can be disappointed with my act," says Paul Hyu, of England, who as "ChineseElvis" uses the

JEFF JOCHIM AND HIS DOG ELVIS JUNIOR.

IRAQI EXPATRIATE, BENJAMIN NISSAN, VOTING IN IRAQ'S 2005 INDEPENDENT ELECTION.

ANNIE LENOX AND DAVE STEWARD OF THE EURHYTHMICS AT THE 1984 GRAMMY AWARDS.

CLOSET ELVIS — ANNIE LENNOX
When she was still with the Eurythmics, Lennox performed at the Grammy Awards ceremony in a '50s Elvis-style wig and sideburns.

JANIE RIOS, ASSISTANT PRINCIPAL AT UNIVERSITY HILLS ELEMENTARY SCHOOL IN NEW MEXICO, SINGS "JAILHOUSE ROCK" TO HER STUDENTS.

persona of Elvis to skewer stereotypes of Asian men. "But what marks them out from other fans, is that they become angry and violent. This is unique to Elvis fans, in my opinion. I think the interesting question regarding these hard-core fans lies in the notion that Elvis has replaced religion for them in a sense. They see anything other than their notion of 'Elvis' as blasphemous."

Barbara Del Piano once put up a poster for a pancreatic cancer benefit performance. The next day she went by, and it was gone, so she put up another—then another, and another, and another. After a bit of investigating, she discovered that they were being pilfered by a local Elvis impersonator. "He drives a cab, and he comes in and he uses the phone and he's ripping this thing down," she said. "He thinks it's blasphemy that a woman puts on the suit and does Elvis." Eventually someone had to tell the poster thief, "This is a cancer benefit, cut it out."

For the most part Belvis has felt welcome among the ranks of her brother Elvises. Occasionally though she feels a bit left out when, for example, the MC at a competition says, "Didn't the guys do a great job? Let's hear it for the guys."

The fact of the matter is, if you are a nontraditional Elvis, you probably will not get the same gigs as the guy who was born with the Elvis look. There is very little chance you'll be hired to play Elvis in the next Elvis biopic and you probably won't be hired by Legends in Concert. Still, there is a niche for you somewhere.

CHAPTER 34
VARIATIONS ON A THEME— FOREIGN ELVISES

Elvis is America's best ever export ... more so than the presidency, more so than the White House, more so than the fast food culture that America has exported. Budweiser is another export that people like, but when you talk about Americana and Betty Boop and Disney, I think Elvis has got to be at the top of the list. Not everybody is an Elvis fan, but if you turn on the radio any place in the world, people will say, "Ah, Elvis Presley."

—MARK LEEN, "EMERALD ELVIS"

It is estimated that more than 40 percent of Elvis's total recorded sales were outside the United States, and Elvis impersonators come from all over the globe as well. ETAs are the only Elvises most non-U.S. residents ever had a chance to see. The only concerts the real Elvis performed outside the United States were in Canada in 1957.

TRIVIA QUESTION: CAN YOU NAME THE THREE CANADIAN CITIES WHERE ELVIS PERFORMED?

ANSWER: *Toronto (Maple Leaf Gardens), Ottawa (Coliseum), and Vancouver (Empire Stadium).*

Sure, being born outside of America is a bit of a drawback if you want to be Elvis. Not only do you have to master the look, the sound, and the moves, but you also have to master English well enough to belt out the lyrics.

Even so, you have the inalienable right to personify The King, and lots of international artists are getting into the game. Some play it every bit as well as the Americans. In 1992, for example, Yasumasa Mori, of Japan, won the International Elvis Impersonator Contest in Memphis, Tennessee, becoming the first non-American to do so.

"I know I don't sound much like Elvis," Mori told the *London Times,* "I certainly don't look like him, but the big Elvis fans chose me because I sing from the bottom of my heart."

According to the *Times,* Mori practiced for twelve years with the dedication of "a Japanese sushi chef who trains for two years just to learn how to boil his rice and another eight to master fish slicing and preparation skills."

The Guinness Book of World Records lists a Belgian as the "most durable Elvis impersonator": Victor Beasley belted out Elvis tunes from 1955 through 2003, a total of forty-nine years—more years than Elvis Presley lived.

Don't you wish you could be like Elvis and give precious gifts to all your friends? When it came to recognizing his supporters, no one had more flash than The King. He gave away thousands of dollars worth of jewels and dozens of cars—usually Cadillacs.

FIFTEEN-YEAR-OLD JUSTIN LIM, FROM HONG KONG, PERFORMS IN FRONT OF ABOUT 800 FANS AT "ELVIS FOREVER IN ASIA" IN TOKYO.

EILERT PILARM, ELVIS EXTRAORDINAIRE

Eilert Pilarm has been amazing international audiences by performing as The King while completely failing to either look or sound like Elvis Presley. To make things even more entertaining, his English is virtually nonexistent, so he sings with joyful abandon unconstrained by the meaning of the lyrics. His "Jailhouse Rock," says Joe Hagan in the *New York Times*, "boggles the mind with its originality." For all of these reasons, Pilarm has become something of an international cult figure in the spirit of "American Idol" reject William Hung. On his Swedish-language Web page, Pilarm offers for sale no less than five CDs, including a "Greatest Hits" compilation.

JAPANESE PRIME MINISTER JUNICHIRO KOIZUMI.

CLOSET ELVIS—JAPANESE PRIME MINISTER JUNICHIRO KOIZUMI

In 2002, the prime minister of the land that invented karaoke released a CD called **Junichiro Koizumi Presents My Favorite Elvis Songs.** He once publicly sang Elvis Presley's "I Want You, I Need You, I Love You" with Tom Cruise.

TIP FOR THE INTERNATIONAL ELVIS: HAVE SOMEONE WHO SPEAKS ENGLISH WELL EXPLAIN SOME OF THE LYRICS TO YOU. THEY SHOULD BE FLUENT ENOUGH TO BE ABLE TO ROUGHLY TRANSLATE SUCH PHRASES AS "HUNKA HUNKA BURNIN' LOVE." (DON'T TAKE THE LYRICS TOO LITERALLY; AMERICANS DON'T GO AROUND DRAGGING TEDDY BEARS ON LEASHES EITHER—IT'S A METAPHOR.)

AFTER YOU HAVE AN IDEA WHAT THE SONG IS TALKING ABOUT, HAVE YOUR FRIEND BREAK DOWN THE WORDS PHONETICALLY AND, IF YOUR LANGUAGE USES A DIFFERENT ALPHABET, WRITE OUT THOSE SOUNDS IN YOUR FAMILIAR CHARACTERS.

TIP

LONMAY

ABOVE: IAN HAINEY ENTERING THE VILLAGE OF LONMAY.

INTERNATIONAL ELVIS TRIVIA: The Scottish town of Lonmay claims to be the "ancestral homeland" of Elvis. A Scottish author traced The King's roots back to the town. Parish records show that Elvis ancestor Andrew Presley married Elspeth Leg in Lonmay in 1713. Their son, Andrew, Jr., moved to America and is the immigrant ancestor of the Presley clan. The town had planned to celebrate the connection by renaming its hotel "Heartbreak Hotel" but they got a stern warning from Graceland about possible trademark violations.

CHAPTER 35
THE GENEROSITY OF ELVIS ON AN ELVIS IMPERSONATOR'S BUDGET

> It didn't matter to him if you were the poorest of poor, the richest of the rich, he treated everyone equally; and that may be why people try to do what they do. I wish I could tribute him in more ways than just performing.
>
> —DON OBUSEK, PITTSBURGH-BASED ETA

The first Cadillac he gave away was a 1954 convertible as a gift to Sam Phillips, of Sun records. In 1973, he spent $200,000 on twenty-nine cars in a week and a half. His pièce de résistance came on July 27, 1975, when he gifted fourteen Caddies in a single day, including one to a stranger, Mennie L. Person, an African-American bank teller who just happened to be at the dealership, window-shopping with her family, when the rock star showed up. (Oprah, eat your heart out!)

If you are a full-time Elvis tribute artist, your means are probably a bit more modest than Elvis's. You're not going to be giving cars away en masse. That doesn't mean you can't honor the spirit of giving that Elvis personified. Let's put his giving into perspective. In 1974, Elvis made $3,508,332 on concerts and record royalties.* That's not even counting the profits he had left over from previous years or the hundreds of thousands of dollars he made from concert appearances

in the early months of 1975. But only counting the $3.5 million, the fourteen Cadillacs were about 17 percent of Elvis's income. Still generous by any measure.

If you make $28,000 a year, you need to give away $4,760 to match Elvis's most famous spending spree. That's just a little bit more than the cost of one really good Elvis costume.

*About $14,551,694 in today's currency.

> Some would argue that Elvis is whatever you take him to be, and that is what makes him available to so many types of performers. I'm more inclined to say that there is something about Elvis that remains constant to his various interpretations and that would be a certain guilelessness, a certain humility, a certain love of performance, of self-expression, and again that exuberance that breaks down boundaries between class, gender, and ethnic identity.

—JEREMY WALLACH, ASSISTANT PROFESSOR, DEPARTMENT OF POPULAR CULTURE, BOWLING GREEN STATE UNIVERSITY

CHAPTER 36
ELVIS
IN SPIRIT—HUMILITY

Some of the greatest violence done to Elvis's image in the years since his death has been by impersonators who adopt the outward trappings of Elvis's persona without paying tribute to his winking sense of humor.

Many tribute artists focus on the moments when Elvis seemed to take himself most seriously—crooning a ballad while wearing a cape. There is a lot of inherent humor in that, but it's not what Elvis was all about.

It only takes a few viewings of the real Elvis to see that his sexiest moments are also his most self-depreciating. The "dangerous" young Elvis took delight in the effect he created. He played with the audience, always with an expression that said, "I can't believe I'm getting away with this."

As he got older and highlighted his serious side, he never completely stopped laughing at himself, at least not until drugs and depression took their toll in his last years. A careful study of the "Aloha from Hawaii" special reveals that Elvis especially had trouble taking himself seriously as a sex symbol. He was tickled by the scarf routine and he could hardly get through the bumps and grinds of "Fever" without laughing. That's what the fans loved about him.

An Elvis who took himself seriously would never have been a star. An Elvis impersonator who takes himself seriously is just sad.

AN ELVIS WHO TOOK HIMSELF TOO SERIOUSLY WOULD NEVER HAVE BEEN A STAR.

CHAPTER 37
VIVA LAS VEGAS!
HOW TO BECOME A WEDDING CHAPEL ELVIS

Some chapels don't treat weddings seriously. They're giving Elvis a bad name.

—KENT RIPLEY, OF GRACELAND WEDDING CHAPEL, QUOTED IN THE *WASHINGTON POST*, MAY 2001

perform a wedding as long as he or she had active charge of a congregation for at least three years) and never have been convicted of a felony, although the ACLU blocked plans by the county clerk to institute a criminal background check of wedding chapel ministers that would determine if they met this last qualification or not.

Norm Jones, ordained by the nondenominational Fellowship of Hope, has been performing Elvis and weddings at the Graceland Wedding Chapel for years, but he doesn't do both at once. He will perform as Elvis and then perform a non-Elvis wedding ceremony, or he will perform a wedding renewal while in Elvis gear. He explained his reluctance to do weddings in the persona of Elvis to a reporter from the *Press Telegram:* "Getting married is a very serious thing. I don't want them to be having an argument someday and one of them say, 'Well, I don't even feel married to you because Elvis did it.'"

If it is your dream to sing the "Hawaiian Wedding Song" after a teary-eyed couple says "I do," there are a few things you should know:

There is a common misconception about Las Vegas Elvis weddings—in most cases, Elvis does not perform the actual ceremony. Elvis (in the form of an impersonator) performs a song or two, witnesses the ceremony, or gives the bride away.

Chapter 122 of the Nevada Revised Statutes governs the issuance of Certificates of Permission to Perform Marriages. You may perform marriages if you are a Supreme Court justice (to the best of our knowledge this would not apply to any Elvis impersonators), a district judge, justice of the peace, municipal judge, or commissioner or deputy commissioner of civil marriages. For the most part, these are not the folks working at wedding chapels.

Interestingly, the city that built an entire industry around its relaxed laws for getting married has slightly more stringent laws than many other states as to what type of minister can perform those weddings. For the record, if you want the right to perform weddings as a minister, the state of Nevada requires more than a simple ordination. You to must perform actual church services (a retired minister can

SIX DEGREES OF ELVIS:

Charlotte Richards, who owns the Special Memory Wedding Chapel, which offers Elvis weddings, arranged the flowers for Elvis Presley's wedding, and her husband shot the photos.

Of course, if a couple doesn't feel sufficiently married by Elvis, they can always renew their vows in Las Vegas at a drive-up wedding chapel window.

So the good news is, you don't have to be a minister to be involved in weddings in Las Vegas. There is definitely a demand for Elvis at Las Vegas wedding chapels, and there is no shortage of weddings—in all, about 5 percent of all weddings performed in the United States each year take place in a county that accounts for less than .5 percent of the nation's population. The wedding industry contributes about $1 billion to the tourist economy of Las Vegas.

The bad news is that there is also an ample supply of Wedding Chapel Elvises. Don't quit your day job and expect to make a fortune in the Vegas wedding biz. You're just as likely to end up hocking your American Eagle jumpsuit for next month's rent—or four months rent, for that matter. At least you can take comfort in the fact that there will be another aspiring Elvis in Vegas to buy it.

VEGAS WEDDINGS BY THE NUMBERS

22—The number of pages in the Las Vegas phone book devoted to listings and advertisements for the wedding industry

50—The estimated number of entertainers in Las Vegas who make at least some money each year impersonating Elvis

350—The average number of marriage licenses processed each day in Clark County

45,000—The number of couples who have their marriage vows renewed in Las Vegas each year

1,731—The number of licenses processed over a two-day period on Valentines Day, 2005

126,000—The number of couples that tie the knot in Clark County, Nevada (i.e., Vegas) each year

TRIVIA QUESTION: ELVIS AND LAS VEGAS ARE FOREVER LINKED. SURPRISINGLY, THE FIRST TIME ELVIS PERFORMED IN LAS VEGAS IN 1956, HE WAS A COMPLETE FLOP. WITHIN DAYS OF HIS OPENING, ELVIS'S NAME WAS DROPPED BELOW THE OTHER PERFORMERS WHO SHARED THE BILL WITH HIM. WHO WERE THEY?

ANSWER: *Shecky Green and the Freddie Martin Band.*

CHAPTER 38
STAGE FRIGHT

I've never gotten over what they call stage fright. I go through it every show. I'm pretty concerned, I'm pretty much thinking about the show. I never get completely comfortable with it, and I don't let the people around me get comfortable with it, in that I remind them that it's a new crowd out there, it's a new audience, and they haven't seen us before. So it's got to be like the first time we go on.

—ELVIS PRESLEY

You've rehearsed with videos, in front of the mirror, and even in front of your mom. You've got the moves down, the vibrato is perfect, and the moves are smooth, but just before you take the stage, bless my soul, what's wrong with you?

Your breathing becomes shallow and you're standing backstage with sweaty palms, shaking hands, and butterflies in the stomach.

Sometimes your gut feelings go beyond butterflies. Stress can make you throw up or run to the bathroom with cramps or diarrhea.

It's all normal. If you don't feel a rush of adrenaline, commonly known as "stage fright," before going up in front of a crowd, check your pulse, you may be dead.

If you want evidence that Elvis himself suffered from stage fright, listen to a recording of *Live in Las Vegas,* which captured Presley's return to live performing after a six-year absence. One little-known factoid about Elvis is that he had a slight stutter that appeared when he was nervous. It is on full display in the chatter between songs on the night of his Las Vegas debut.

The key to defeating stage fright is not to overcome the nervous sensations—you won't. You just need to learn to love them. Think of it as excitement rather than fear. And remember, tribute artist audiences are a forgiving lot. The most important thing is to have a good time. It will be contagious.

"Most of the people who come to shows wouldn't recognize a good Elvis if you dropped it in front of them," says ETA Jerome Martin. "Elvis music is Elvis music to them. As long as he's up there, he's gyrating, he's having fun. It's the excitement of live entertainment."

ARE THEY LAUGHING *AT* YOU OR LAUGHING *WITH* YOU?

After months of preparation and practice to perfect those Elvis moves, sounds, and mannerisms you're ready to take to the stage. You make your grand entrance in your exact-replica Red Eagle jumpsuit, and along with the cheers you hear laughter and titters. Are they snickers of joy or ridicule? Are they laughing *at* you or laughing *with* you? I won't sugarcoat it—it's a little of both. When people book an Elvis tribute artist, they know they're going to have a good time. If the ETA is good, they'll enjoy the act because of the charisma of the performer. If he or she is bad, they know they'll have a laugh. That's why Elvis impersonators are so popular: you can't lose.

"You may very much be pursuing a calling to keep this tradition alive," says Robert Thompson, past president of the International Popular Culture Association and director of the Center for the Study of Popular Television at Syracuse University, "but in many ways that tradition is subsidized by

a large number of audience members who are there to just have a rip-roaring kitschy good time. And I suppose that's true of a lot of artists. People who do dinner theater are serious actors who want to interpret a role and give a great performance and they're subsidized by people in the audience who want to see a play, eat some prime rib and talk to whoever is at the table during the play."

As the performer, it's up to you to tip the scales one way or the other. One of the greatest skills an Elvis tribute artist must learn, especially a late-period Elvis artist, is to overwhelm your audience with enough good feeling and enough of your own humor to win them over. You want to *share* the joke *with*, not *be* the joke *for* the audience. The best in the biz make the audience take itself less seriously so that everybody has a great time.

There are about 35,000 Elvis impersonators in America right now and you don't need that many—that's for sure.

—BRIAN SIMPSON, CANADA-BASED ETA

Rule number 4: Don't quit your day job.

Now that you've decided to take Elvising to the next level and perform professionally, where do you start? Chances are, your first gig will not be at a Las Vegas casino. The problem with the Elvis profession is the same as with the oldest profession—too many enthusiastic amateurs. With so many Elvises out there, it is hard to stand out among the bejeweled, gyrating crowd.

"When Elvis impersonation really hit the big time right after Elvis died, these guys were signing three-million-dollar contracts to perform with the casinos," says Brian Simpson. "Now you won't make five hundred dollars a week."

Instead, look for smaller venues: local events and businesses that may need to be Elvised up. Scan your paper for a "Grand Opening" and try to contact the proprietor. An appearance by "Elvis" is a great way for a new business to get some attention and create a festive mood. Nursing homes, school events, parades, local fairs, and private parties are all good places to get started.

The important thing to remember is—no matter how small the event may seem—you should always give it 100 percent, as you never know who is going to be there. If you act put-out to be wasting your talents on the local Little League championship party, you may make enemies of quite a few parents, any of whom might have otherwise recommended you to someone else. Be professional and courteous with everyone, whether you're in costume or not, and pass out as many business cards as you can.

Corollary: Don't run off to Vegas.

Las Vegas may seem like Mecca for Elvis artists but be forewarned, you will be a tiny fish in an ocean of Elvises. As Las Vegas historian Hal Rothman explained, it's not that they have unemployed Elvises everywhere, but, "We have a lot of Elvises who are unemployed as Elvis. They are employed as something else."

Mark Leen, "Emerald Elvis," believes aspiring Elvises are better off in Europe than in America. "People talk about the freedoms of America; I disagree," he says. "I think a lot of people in America in my profession are abused. They're working for $150 a night, having to sing for three or four hours a night just to say 'I played Vegas.' They've been deluded and conned by ruthless businessmen in the same way that they sell 'you can win the mega bucks on the machine' to the fools that go in and put the money in. That's an unfortunate part of Americana."

Put another way: Think globally, Elvis locally.

TRIVIA QUESTION: IN 2001, *FORBES* PUBLISHED A LIST OF THE WEALTHIEST DEAD CELEBRITIES (THE CELEBRITIES WHOSE ESTATES CONTINUE TO EARN THE MOST). ELVIS PRESLEY TOPPED THE LIST. WHO WERE THE RUNNERS UP?

ANSWER: *Elvis was followed by (2) Charles Shulz, (3) John Lennon, (4) Dr. Seuss, and (5) Jimi Hendrix.*

J.D. FORTUNE OF INXS.

CLOSET ELVIS — J.D. FORTUNE

J. D. Fortune, who was chosen to be the new lead singer of INXS in the reality TV series **Rock Star: INXS,** was once an Elvis impersonator. He performed as both Elvis and Buddy Holly in **Legends, A Tribute to the Superstars,** in Ontario, Canada.

CHAPTER 40
KEEPING IT LEGAL

In general, impersonating Elvis falls under First Amendment freedom of expression, whether one is good or bad at impersonating him, whether one is making a sincere effort to pay tribute to him or doing an unflattering parody. There are some potential commercial activities of Elvis impersonators that can go beyond their broad First Amendment rights and get into [Elvis Presley Enterprise's] Elvis trademark rights, and there we have a problem to deal with from time to time with one impersonator or another. There's also a lot of gray area to wade through in an individual's First Amendment rights versus EPE's trademark rights. But, in general, EPE and the Elvis impersonator population live peacefully but apart in the world of Elvis.

—OFFICIAL STATEMENT OF ELVIS PRESLEY ENTERPRISES ON ELVIS IMPERSONATORS,
AS IT APPEARS ON THE OFFICIAL ELVIS WEB SITE, ELVIS.COM

✦✦
✦✦
✦✦
✦✦

Who owns Elvis? That, of course, is a deep philosophical question. The fans could be said to "own" Elvis—his memory, his spirit—as much as anyone else. Elvis, the feeling, the concept, belongs to all of us. But that is not a legal answer. Legally speaking, the owner of Elvis Presley—his likeness, name, and image—is Elvis Presley Enterprises. (But even from a legal standpoint that is an oversimplification—intellectual property and trademark issues are ever evolving in the world's courts.)

So what exactly is Elvis Presley Enterprises? Right now, Robert Sillerman, who created the SFX radio empire, owns 85 percent of the Elvis estate. He bought Elvis for $100 million in 2004. Priscilla Presley remains an "executive consultant," and Lisa Marie, Elvis's only heir, gets to keep the palace (Graceland), and most of Elvis's personal effects. The Elvis estate took in $44.9 million in 2003.

Someone could, and no doubt has, written a whole book on how intellectual property rights have been interpreted and how it affects ownership of the legacy of Elvis—and your right to tribute or parody him. For our purposes, you just need to know that EPE holds various U.S. rights to Elvis Presley, including four trademarks: Elvis, Elvis Presley, Elvis Presley's Memphis, and Elvis Presley's Heartbreak Hotel. When you name your tribute show, keep that in mind, unless you want to find yourself in a hunka-hunka burning lawsuit. Generally speaking, a person is safe doing a tribute to Elvis as long as he or she does not claim to *be* Elvis. The issue is whether someone is likely to be confused and assume that you are Elvis or officially representing Elvis.

Intellectual property is fraught with exceptions and shades of gray, but the more you are aware of the Elvis estate's commercial interests, and the more you try to avoid stepping on their toes, the safer you will be. If you're worried about it, bill your show as a "Tribute to The King." The term "The King" belongs to no one.

There is another issue you need to keep in mind. Whenever someone performs music, the composer is entitled to royalties for its use—unless it is old enough to be in the public domain, which would not apply to many of Elvis's songs. (Some gospel songs and old standards might be in the public domain, but it would make for a strange Elvis show.) If you use backing tracks, be sure you are buying the performance license along with the recording. Even though it is unlikely that the music police will walk into your gig in Fergus Falls, Minnesota, and ask to see your license, they theoretically could. To stay within the bounds of the law, be sure you have your licensed CDs or cassettes on hand, even if you've made a dub of them to mix them into your set list.

I AM ELVIS. NO, REALLY. I *AM* ELVIS.

No one can stop you from claiming to be "Elvis" if that is actually your name. That said, there aren't many true Elvises around. In 1935, the year Elvis Presley was born, "Elvis" was the 798th most popular name for boys in the country (in other words, about .006 percent of the male population were Elvises). It was only slightly more popular than Chuck (as its own name, not short for Charles) and Errol, but less popular than Elwyn, Denzil, Edsel, and Aloysius.

In 1977, the year of Elvis's death, the name had moved up to number 598 in popularity (between Buddy and Torrey). About .011 percent of the male children born that year were Elvises. In 2004, however, it had dipped down to being the 694th most popular baby boy's name.

RESOURCE GUIDE